"Many people of faith have written about their personal cancer experience but very few caregivers have described their own struggle through this health minefield. Cyndi Siegfried writes with clarity and profundity as she unfolds her journey with doctors, her faith and the husband she loves, seeking the best healthcare possible while growing closer to her Lord on the way. This is a must read for caregivers starting down such a tortuous road with any serious illness."

—Al Weir, M.D., oncologist
Vice President of Campus and
Community Ministries of The Christian Medical and
Dental Associations, author of *When Your Doctor Has Bad News*

"Like millions of people around the world, I've watched close family members struggle with the terrible disease of cancer. Cynthia has written an inspirational book about her experience with the disease. The revelations she shares about her role as Jim's caregiver will provide hope to anyone in the midst of an ordeal with cancer and someone they love."

—Jason Sehorn
analyst for CBS College Sports network, former defensive back for New York Giants and St. Louis Rams. Jason married Angie Harmon in 2001, following his proposal to her on the Tonight Show with Jay Leno.

"For years Cynthia Siegfried has undertaken a task no one wants to acquire: caregiver for a loved one with cancer. Now, the lessons she's learned will ease your caregiving as she shares her practical pointers and God's precious promises. If you need encouragement, I encourage you to read this book."

—Lynn Eib
cancer survivor, patient advocate
and author of the bestseller *When God & Cancer Meet*

"Finally a book that addresses the caregiver. After my two cancer battles, I look back and wonder how my dear sweet husband did it.

How did he hold up under the pressure of taking care of me as well as my three boys? As a cancer survivor I know the support thrown our way was directed at me. But I know he needed support through prayer and friendship too. Talking about a crisis does help. Putting a book in print to help the caregiver is a wonderful idea!"

—Brenda Ladun, cancer survivor
Birmingham newscaster, author of *Getting Better, Not Bitter*

CANCER JOURNEY

Cynthia Siegfried

Psalm 91: 4-7

CANCER JOURNEY

A CAREGIVER'S VIEW FROM THE PASSENGER SEAT

CYNTHIA ZAHM SIEGFRIED

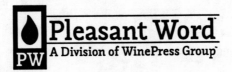

Pleasant Word (a division of WinePress Publishing, PO Box 428, Enumclaw, WA 98022) functions only as book publisher. As such, the ultimate design, content, editorial accuracy, and views expressed or implied in this work are those of the author.

Unless otherwise noted, all Scriptures are taken from the *Holy Bible, New International Version®, NIV®*. Copyright © 1973, 1978, 1984 by Biblica, Inc.™ Used by permission of Zondervan. All rights reserved worldwide.

ISBN 13: 978-1-4141-1549-8
ISBN 10: 1-4141-1549-0
Library of Congress Catalog Card Number: 2009907396

Jim,
> My inspiration, my hero, my soul-mate, in sickness and health 'til death do us part.

Ashleigh, Tara, and Nicole,
> If I had known how well you were going to turn out, I would have had three more.

CONTENTS

Introduction   xi

1. Kidnapped   1
2. A Jerky Start   15
3. On the Road   29
4. The Road to the Crazy House   41
5. A Detour—Exploring My Faith   49
6. Fuel for Body and Spirit—God's Provisions   59
7. Streams in the Desert   69
8. The Endless Journey   81
9. Running on Empty in the Valley of
       the Shadow of Death   93
10. Last Man Standing   103
11. Leaving a Roadmap   113

The Caregiver's GPS   125
Endnotes   129
Resources and Recommended Reading   135

INTRODUCTION

O N THE DAY my husband, Jim, was diagnosed with cancer, we began a journey that changed us forever. I was just a passenger, along for the ride, but I was profoundly affected by the illness. Being caregiver to a seriously ill person has problems different from, but equally as serious as, those of the patient. Unfortunately, support for the caregiver is often lacking.

Almost two million people in the United States will be diagnosed with cancer this year. Most will be cared for by family and friends. This book is for you—the husbands, wives, children, parents, and friends who are providing care for a loved one with a devastating illness.

I invite you to accompany me as I share the fears and joys, struggles and triumphs encountered on the ride of a lifetime. Hopefully, my map will provide a shortcut, taking you from the terror of diagnosis, through the fear of recurrence, and finally to a place of peace and acceptance.

Jim frequently says cancer is harder on the caregiver than on the patient. I don't believe that for a minute. One thing, though, is certain. The view from the passenger seat is different, and bound to be more difficult—if you don't know the Driver!

CHAPTER 1

KIDNAPPED

*If all the difficulties were known at the outset of a
long journey, most of us would never start out at all.*
—Dan Rather

THE DAY STARTED like any other. The sun rose in
the east. The morning paper landed in the drive. The
alarm rang at seven. I fortified myself with a shot
of Dr Pepper and set out for a morning walk through my
quiet neighborhood. I didn't bother to turn around when
the car pulled up behind me.

He grabbed me quickly, his arm around my neck, hand
over my mouth. I fought and screamed to no avail as he
threw me roughly into the back of the car. He only had to hit
me once to get my attention. I stopped my futile struggling
as he taped my wrists and ankles.

"Who are you? What do you want with me?" I cried.

He answered in a language I had never heard before. I had no idea where he was taking me or why.

"God help me," I sobbed.

My cancer journey had begun.

We were at a good point in our lives.

Our three daughters were educated and happily married. We had five grandchildren and our youngest daughter, Ashleigh, and her husband, Chris, had just announced they were expecting their first baby. My husband, Jim, was at the pinnacle of his career in the brokerage industry. He had just been elected deacon chairman of our 15,000-member church. Neither of us had any health problems. We were happily ensconced in a beautiful neighborhood, living the American dream. We didn't know the dream was about to become a nightmare.

On Friday, November 1, after a routine physical by a new internist, Dr. Mark Castellaw, the doctor reported that Jim's cholesterol was a bit high, and that he saw a couple of spots he "didn't like the looks of" on the chest X-ray. We weren't too concerned about either finding. After all, the cholesterol could easily be controlled and the spots were probably artifacts or scar tissue from numerous respiratory infections during childhood. Jim was a runner and former college basketball player, had never smoked, and was feeling perfectly well. Just to be safe, the doctor scheduled an appointment for him to have an MRI the following week. We went on with business as usual.

For Jim, business as usual meant fifty-hour work weeks, lengthy church meetings, coaching our grandsons' basketball teams, and playing tennis. He ran about five miles a day, before dawn, and farther on weekends. For me, business as usual meant Bible studies, tennis matches, coaching a country club swim team, and a part-time job in a local boutique. We approached fun and business with the same intensity.

On Thursday, November 7, Jim went for his "no big deal" MRI. The next night as we were preparing to do some early Christmas shopping, we received a phone call from Dr. Castellaw to tell Jim he was sending his MRI to a pulmonologist for review because it showed a small shadow in the left lung. He said it might be nothing, but he preferred not to ignore it.

"How refreshing," I thought, "to have a doctor actually make a personal phone call on the weekend." We went on with our plans for the evening, unalarmed and oblivious to the impending cataclysm.

I woke up Tuesday knowing Jim had an appointment with the pulmonologist, but I wasn't terribly concerned—at least, not concerned enough to go with him. After all, I had plenty to do in preparation for the upcoming holidays and for my tennis trip later in the week. I needed to go to Tuesday Morning to buy a telescope for the grandsons, then on to Stein Mart where I worked one day a week.

I had just returned from lunch when Jim called. I could tell from his voice something was wrong. "The pulmonologist wants me to go to The West Clinic for a biopsy," he said in a strained voice. In Memphis, The West Clinic is synonymous with cancer. I rushed from Stein Mart without even punching the clock and drove home, trying to calm myself down.

Jim came home from work, a rare happening, since he'd long labored under the notion that Wall Street would crash if he wasn't sitting at his desk for the opening and closing bells. We made calls to set up the biopsy appointment. We prayed. We talked. We rationalized.

"The doctor is probably just being cautious."

"You've never smoked."

"It's probably just scar tissue."

"I've had spots in my breast that turned out to be nothing."

We spent three hours trying to coordinate the lung capacity test and the biopsy, which were both to be scheduled for the following morning. I actually expected the clinic to fit him in that very day or surely the next morning. I pleaded with the receptionist, then the nurse. I had no idea we were among hundreds in Memphis alone who were trying to schedule biopsies that very day. "Do they actually expect us to wait around for forty-eight hours with a suspicious spot in his lung?" I thought. Besides, I wanted the test completed so I could go to my tennis tournament unencumbered by guilt or worry. We needed the test done immediately so as not to interfere with my plans.

There was a time when I truly believed that without my organization and worrying skills, my family could not function. Like a puppeteer, I worked the strings that kept life flowing smoothly. My daughters said I had a need for control that was out of control. With the help of God and a good psychologist, I thought I had mellowed over the years and learned to "let go and let God." But in this situation, I felt my hands finding their comfortable place on my well-worn reins of control.

Perhaps because I sounded so desperate, the clinic agreed to squeeze Jim in the next morning for a needle biopsy. For me, the scheduling of the test was paramount. With that accomplished, I moved ahead full-speed, believing I could get the negative results by Thursday morning and be on the road with my tennis team by Thursday afternoon. My life would go on with just a minor interruption.

The next morning we reported to the hospital for the lung capacity test which went extremely well. I was reassured. Then we headed with Ashleigh and Tara, our middle daughter, for the biopsy. I'm sure everyone recognized us as novices. We had our Bibles, *Vogue*, *People*, several books, four cell phones and a small entourage of friends and family.

At the clinic we spoke with a doctor for the first time since the call from Dr. Castellaw. The radiologist was very helpful in explaining exactly what would happen in the procedure.

"There are three visible spots, the largest about a centimeter in diameter," he told us. "I don't think we are seeing a granuloma (a harmless group of cells), but we won't know for certain until we have the biopsy results. Twenty percent of lung cancers occur in non-smokers," he continued. "If Jim is among that twenty percent, his overall health will be in his favor."

I think the radiologist was trying to prepare me for bad news, but I just didn't get it. I ignored any part of the conversation I didn't want to hear and focused on the statistics for non-smokers and lung cancer. At the time, I somehow thought those were good odds.

"The procedure will be difficult to perform," he warned, "because of the location and size of the tumors and there is always a risk of collapsing the lung."

A collapsed lung? Now he had my attention. I was no longer worried about whether Jim had cancer. After all, the chances were slim. I forgot about cancer and started worrying about the biopsy procedure rather than the biopsy results. I was so pitifully ignorant of what a cancer diagnosis would mean that I didn't have sense enough to worry about the results instead of the test.

As they prepared Jim for the procedure, we prayed together in the adjacent hallway. "Please, Lord, guide the doctor's hands right to the tiny tumor. Don't let the lung collapse. Keep him safe." I didn't know that in a week a collapsed lung would be the least of our worries.

The biopsy was successful. That is, the technician was able to hit the largest of the tumors and withdraw enough fluid for analysis. The lung didn't collapse and by afternoon we were on our way home, relieved that the whole thing was over. Jim was none the worse for the wear and he fully intended to go to work the next day—business as usual. I was thinking we might get some results by morning, the day I was to leave for my tournament. I briefly considered not going until after we heard the results.

"Don't be ridiculous," Jim said. "I'll be at the office and you'll be home alone waiting for the phone to ring, with what will probably be good news anyway."

So I set off on Thursday afternoon with Sharon Schulter, my friend and tennis partner, for an eight-hour drive across the state. When Jim didn't get a call by Thursday night, I thought, "No news is good news. Surely if they had found anything troubling they would have called immediately. I mean, they wouldn't just let someone walk around with lung cancer, right?"

Friday, November 15, my fifty-sixth birthday, would prove to be the most memorable. After our second match, the team went for lunch. Just when I had placed an order, my cell phone chirped "Take Me Out to the Ballgame," indicating it was Jim calling. I snatched it up, hoping for good news but bracing myself for bad. I had difficulty hearing him with the chatter at the table. With my finger in one ear and a sinking feeling in the pit of my stomach, I jumped up from the table and walked into the nearby bar area.

"Can you hear me?" he said. "It's cancer."

There aren't words to describe the emotions those words evoke. My knees crumbled and I collapsed into the nearest booth. Everything stopped as adrenaline pumped through my body. I began to tremble and didn't stop trembling for three months. When you are faced with a life-changing event, it feels as if everything you've ever done, or will ever do, pivots on that single moment in time.

On Thursday I had thought, "No news is good news." On Friday, I learned that "no news is—no news."

Jim received the call from the doctor around noon, but once he heard the word "cancer" he didn't hear anything else the doctor said. By the time he had a chance to recover enough from the initial shock to ask questions, there was no one available to answer them. I think newly diagnosed cancer patients should be assigned an advocate to shepherd them and answer questions at this critical time. Unfortunately, most have an experience similar to ours. Someone drops a hand grenade into your life and you are left to pick up the pieces.

Our oldest daughter, Nicole, had already begun her Internet search for information about lung cancer. However, her search was impeded because Jim couldn't remember what the doctor had told him. Was it small cell? Non-small cell? Operable? Inoperable?

Even if Jim had not been stricken temporarily mindless, I doubt the words the doctor used would have registered with him. He didn't know an adenocarcinoma from an adenoid. He knew he had lungs and that they were necessary, but certainly not much beyond that.

On the long trip home from the tennis tournament, Sharon drove while I made phone calls to family and friends. Most reflected my response: disbelief, fear, sadness. For those who didn't have medical experience, either as a patient or a professional, the very mention of cancer was enough to strike fear in their hearts.

Those who knew something about lung cancer, in particular, were appropriately concerned and offered what would prove to be sage advice. My friends, Susan and Warren Crain, both with medical backgrounds, suggested we call MD Anderson, a major comprehensive cancer center in Houston, Texas, to set up an appointment. *That's an overreaction,* I thought. I didn't really want to set out cross-country into unfamiliar territory to take care of this problem. Little did I know I was already engaged in a journey during which nothing would be familiar. We had entered a foreign country in which we were expected to find our way, with no map, when we didn't even speak the language.

Our daughter called me several times and judiciously reported some of the information she had gathered, still not knowing how much of it applied to Jim. She must already have suspected what I was to learn in the next few weeks: this was serious business.

On Monday, November 18, Jim began a series of appointments with various specialists. "I am so afraid," I wrote in my journal that day. "What if I hear something spoken or implied that sends my hope plummeting?" I had never been afraid to go to an appointment with a doctor because none of us had ever had a serious health problem. I loved checking the column of "no's" on the health history—as if that somehow protected me from any ailment or disease.

The first appointment was with the pulmonologist, Dr. Gary Trew, who answered questions, perhaps too honestly. He was "optimistic for a cure" but warned that we wouldn't know what other areas might be affected until after the PET scan on Thursday.

"What's that?" I asked.

"A PET scan," he explained, "is designed to show malignancies in the body. Jim will be injected with a radioactive sugar solution. The cancerous tissue absorbs more of this agent than the healthy cells do. When the radiologist runs the special scanner over his body, the abnormal masses will light up."

I finally began to see the grim reality of the situation when Dr. Trew said, "This is a difficult surgery, sometimes fatal," and that we should "have our affairs in order." In the elevator, after the appointment, Jim and I clung to each other.

We went directly from the doctor's office to the attorney's. We had made a will several years before, having put off the unpleasant task much longer than we should have. Making a will was a job I found depressing and anxiety-provoking, even under good circumstances. When we made the will, our deaths were unlikely events relegated to a place in the faraway future. Since death had leapt disobligingly from its appointed place in time, I needed to re-examine the provisions we had made. I wanted to know exactly what would happen in the event of Jim's death, now that we were talking in particulars rather than vagaries.

This was a terrifying prospect for me. *Would there be enough money for me to live on? How could I possibly get along without my husband?* I had never paid a bill. I didn't know what bank had our mortgage. I was a spoiled child who had never had to worry about any aspect of our finances. I needed to know what would happen if he died on the operating table at fifty-six rather than in his rocker at the old folks home at ninety-six.

That day was one of the most difficult in our early journey. Hearing the word "cancer" is not easy, but initially we were protected by our ignorance. Gradually, God was illuminating the road before us, one curve at a time. I went to bed that night with a heavy heart.

The next morning I felt even worse. On the way to meet the surgeon, we prayed God would put people in our path who would encourage us, and that the surgeon wouldn't say anything we couldn't bear to hear. God answered our prayers with compassionate nurses and medical professionals.

The surgeon told us he intended to remove a small part of the left lung and the surrounding lymph nodes. If only one of the three spots on the lung was malignant, the chances of a cure were about eighty percent. If more than one of the three was cancerous, the chances dropped to about seventy percent.

The surgery was slated for Monday, November 24, and would take about ninety minutes, the surgeon told us. Jim would spend five or six days in the hospital and four weeks home from work. He balked at that. "I have no intention of missing six weeks of work at the end of the fiscal year. That just isn't happening."

Only two weeks had passed since Jim's routine physical and one week since we received the biopsy results. Our world had been turned upside down and I couldn't get it turned upright again. Information—accurate and inaccurate—was coming at us from so many sources that I couldn't begin to process it all.

That night after meeting with the surgeon, an acquaintance called to tell me she had been diagnosed a year earlier with the same kind of cancer as Jim, broncholalveolar carcinoma, or BAC. She said she wasn't expected to live through another Christmas. I had seen this woman at church, bald and ravaged by the cancer, but I had no idea her kind of cancer was like Jim's.

I kept grasping at straws in the conversation trying to find some aspect of her medical history that would differentiate her situation from my husband's. *Had she ever smoked? Maybe she was in poor health before they found the cancer? Maybe she waited too long to see the doctor? Maybe she ate too many charred hamburgers?*

The conversation was devastating. Sitting at the kitchen table in the quiet, evening hours of early winter, I wept. *Would this Christmas be his last? Would he die on the operating table?* I didn't tell Jim about the call. Already I had begun to protect him.

When I woke the next morning, I was humming a song I had heard in church but wasn't really familiar with. I hummed it for my daughter Tara on the phone and she told me the words.

> *Give thanks, with a grateful heart,*
> *Give thanks to the Holy One,*
> *Give thanks, because He's given Jesus Christ, His Son.*
> *And now let the weak say I am strong,*
> *Let the poor say I am rich because of all*
>   *the Lord has done for me,*
> *Give thanks.*[1]

How did that particular song get into my resting brain? I'm sure there is a scientific explanation (as there are for most extrasensory phenomena), but I believe God was telling me how I was to respond to our situation.

The idea of giving thanks in all situations was not new to me. I was familiar with Philippians 4:6-7. "Do not be anxious about anything, but in everything, by prayer and petition, with thanksgiving, present your requests to God. And the peace of God, which transcends all understanding, will guard your hearts and your minds in Christ Jesus."

Years ago I read *The Hiding Place* by Corrie ten Boom and was greatly impressed by her application of this verse during her imprisonment at the Ravensbruck concentration camp in Germany during World War II. A Dutch Christian, ten Boom was part of the underground that helped Jews escape the Nazi regime. She and her entire family were arrested by the Nazis in February, 1944. Her father died just ten days after their arrest; her sister died at Ravensbruck later that year before Corrie's release in December. Throughout her ordeal, she thanked God even for the vermin that plagued the prisoners, believing He was able to bring blessings from that which was meant for evil. He was faithful, because the lice kept the Nazi guards from spending too much time in the barracks, for fear of contamination, thus affording the prisoners more freedom.[2]

I know God still speaks directly to us today—through other Christians, through the Holy Spirit and, of course, through His Word. But this was different. That night was the first time God had spoken directly to me. I needed a reminder in the chaos and panic that had befallen me and God reached down and provided that through this song. If the principle of gratefulness was so important to God that he sent me this message, I figured I should listen. I prayed, "God, I don't know what lies ahead but I know you are with me. I thank you in advance for the good that will come out of this seemingly adverse situation. Like David, I will praise you though my heart is heavy." The next day I went to the bookstore and purchased a CD, *Give Praise*[3], containing the song God put in my heart. It became my theme song throughout the months to follow.

Cancer sneaked up on me, kidnapping my thoughts, emotions, and energy. But, already, God was showing me who was in control.

ADVICE FOR CAREGIVERS

1. Do not ignore exam results—even if the patient exhibits no symptoms.
2. Take a note pad to all initial appointments.
3. Take someone with you for support during tests.
4. Be open about your problem so that others can pray for you.
5. Start praising God for His goodness—even if you don't feel like it.
6. Develop an attitude of thankfulness.

CHAPTER 2

A JERKY START

A journey is like a marriage; the sure way to be
wrong is to think you control it.

—John Steinbeck

MONDAY MORNING CAME, appropriately cold and dreary. Our arrival at the hospital is clear in my mind, although it took place seven years ago. When we walked in, several people were waiting for us and others would come in and out during the day. A friend of mine whose own husband was in treatment for inoperable lung cancer came to offer support, bringing me a book on lung cancer that she had found helpful. I accepted it graciously, while thinking, *What does this have to do with me? After today Jim's lung cancer will be history.* I knew the surgery and recovery would be difficult, but much of my anxiety had been alleviated by the results of the PET scan which, we were told, was ninety percent accurate in detecting malignancies. Since the scan showed nothing except the solitary tumor, I expected them to remove the lower left lobe, stitch him up, and send us on our merry way.

I was eager for Jim to have the operation and get back to normal. Jim, however, became increasingly anxious as the surgery time drew closer. He was fearful about the tube that would remain in his throat in recovery. A friend who worked in thoracic ICU came in while he was being prepped and gave him good advice. "When you awake in the recovery room, if you feel the breathing tube, you must be alive. Start thanking God for bringing you through the surgery." This was an affirmation of the message God had given me—"Give Thanks."

We gathered in the ICU waiting room where the surgeon was to call us when the surgery was over. I had been in that room on several occasions to visit but never while my husband was the one on the operating table. The place takes on an entirely different atmosphere when you are the one waiting for the phone to ring.

Two hours later than we expected, the call came. "Your husband came through the surgery fine," the surgeon reported, "but we found some additional tumors in the upper left lobe and some lymph nodes that look suspicious. I conferred with his pulmonologist and his oncologist while he was on the table and we all agreed that we should leave as much lung as possible to give him the best quality of life. I removed all the visible cancer but the presence of these additional tumors increases the likelihood that there are others in the lung or elsewhere that are too small to detect."

I felt like an elephant was stomping on my diaphragm. Our daughters gathered around me at the phone trying to understand what had gone wrong. I sagged against the wall, unable to get my breath, crying too hard to talk. For the second time in ten days my world was falling apart.

I do not cry daintily. When my emotions, which I usually hold tightly under guard, finally break free, they run alarmingly amok. Rather than a solitary tear sliding down my cheek, bodily fluids run from eyes and nose creating trails of mascara through blotches of rapidly reddening skin. I am not silent. I sob and snort, making it impossible for anyone in the vicinity to ignore my outburst.

I was oblivious to the effect of my emotional display on those around me. Nothing they said calmed me down. I couldn't pray with them and I couldn't listen to reason. I kept repeating as if in shock, "Will he still be able to run?" As the months passed and the disease took its toll, I realized how trivial that worry was.

I pulled myself together to go back to see Jim in recovery. I was hoping he wouldn't be lucid enough to ask me for the report. No such luck. He was surprisingly coherent and immediately asked what they had found. I didn't want to lie to him. "They found some additional tumors but they were able to remove them." (True.) "You're going to be fine." (Maybe not true.)

At this point I began the pattern that would become de rigueur for the rest of the journey. I would be the protector, the encourager, the source and the disseminator of information. Most of the decisions would be mine to make—at first because Jim was too ill, and later, because I had assumed responsibility for his treatment. I jumped into this role unthinkingly because it was necessary, and also because I was the one more interested in matters of health and science. Still, there would be times when I wanted to shed the shackles of responsibility I so willingly accepted that day.

Staying in the hospital is exhausting, especially when the hospitalization is complicated by fear and worry. If someone could have told me Jim was going to be alright, I would have rested easier. I was desperate for reassurance. From the time of the phone conversation in the waiting room with the surgeon, I sensed the prognosis was not good and I needed answers that no one was able or willing to provide. I am not a fly-by-the-seat-of-your-pants kind of girl. My need to know was tied to my need for control.

Because our doctors always brought bad news, I didn't like them—an appraisal that would change over time. When one of them approached the room, I got physically ill because no one could tell me what I wanted to hear—that my husband would recover. Thus began my education in reading between the lines, body language, and tone of voice.

One doctor said, "You have been dealt a tough blow." Translation: *Your reaction to the surgical findings is warranted.*

The oncologist came to the door of the room looking grim. "I'm so sorry." Translation: *I can't offer much hope.*

The surgeon said, "You just have to take the time you've been given and make it count." Translation: *Your husband doesn't have much time left.*

"Great," I said to my daughters. "They think he is going to die."

"No," the girls assured me, "They probably mean you should enjoy the time Dad will spend at home recuperating."

I knew better. Already I had developed a heightened sense of awareness, looking for nuances that might have gone unnoticed a month before. I was picking up information gradually like a rolling snowball picks up unnecessary debris. Bombarded with opinions from every direction, I was unable to sort the good from the bad.

Tara, Nicole, and I took turns sleeping alternately in the chair or on the sofa in the hospital room. The rhythmic whirring of the pump, draining fluid from his lungs, kept me awake most of the time. I prayed for God's help almost without ceasing. I looked at the book my friend had brought me in the waiting room (the one on lung cancer I thought I wouldn't need) and scared myself to death. *Dear God, surely these statistics don't apply to Jim!* Until the pathology reports came back, I didn't even know the extent of the disease, but I did know it was beyond the Stage I we had counted on. "If he had a seventy percent survival rate at Stage I," I reasoned correctly, "it has to be lower now."

Periodically I burst into tears. There were times I wished I could plug myself up to his I.V. and get a good shot of whatever pain-killer they were dispensing. When the I.V. malfunctioned and Dilaudid ran down his arm, I was tempted to lick it up. I never felt comfortable leaving. I wanted to be there when anyone came by with information that might shed some light on what we were facing.

We had barely made it past the jerky start when we encountered the first of many obstacles, the additional cancer found during surgery. In retrospect, I understand that our experience was no different from that of countless others. However, at the time I naively expected the trip to be smooth sailing. I didn't know that at every stop I would have to readjust my expectations along with the course. I had yet to learn that a cancer journey is like the road to Hana in Hawaii—more bumps and curves than I could handle without Dramamine. At least on the Hana trip we had a map and knew what to expect. On a cancer journey you never know what lies ahead.

Only ten days had passed since the day we celebrated the good news from the PET scan; it seemed like ten years. Ironically, leaving the hospital was difficult because I had adjusted to our routine there and found some comfort in the familiarity of the environment. We were insulated in the hospital, protected from whatever beasts were awaiting us outside. I was afraid to go home, afraid to start down a different road. Granted, home was familiar territory, but it had taken on an entirely different perspective because the occupants had been forever altered. My life would never be the same.

My husband just had his chest cut open, a couple of ribs broken and removed, and almost an entire lung excised. I received better instructions when taking home a puppy from the pet store than in taking home a cancer patient from the hospital. I didn't understand a thing about the disease except that it was a very bad one to have. I had the ominous feeling this might be our last Christmas together.

Caregiver fatigue, resulting from staying in the hospital, is a problem for which I still see no solution. When the patient is gravely ill and unable to oversee his own care, you simply cannot depend on an overworked nursing staff to see to his needs. Additionally, there are those in the medical field—as in any other—who are just plain incompetent. I had friends who were willing to stay with Jim but I believed I needed to be there. By the time he came home from the hospital and my real caregiving began, I was physically and emotionally spent from the hospital stay and the whirlwind that preceded it. It is no wonder I felt unable to cope with caring for him.

I had never taken care of anyone who was seriously ill. My grandparents had died suddenly. When my Dad had colon cancer surgery, I was already married and away from home. My children had the usual childhood illnesses, but they were uncomplicated and of short duration.

Nor was I the nurturing, caregiver type. I grew up in a home where no one took to their sick bed unless they were vomiting. Our medicine chest consisted of a small cardboard box in the top of a kitchen cabinet, containing mercurochrome, baby aspirin, calamine lotion, Fletcher's Castoria, and some sort of gooey, multi-purpose, black salve. I don't think we owned a thermometer; my mother used the hand-on-the-forehead method.

I was ill-prepared for the task ahead of me. Jim required around-the-clock care. He was in pain, unable to lie down even to sleep. Away from the confines of the hospital, he was beginning to recognize his limitations and wondering how long they would last. I was doing my best to be positive and protect him from any information that might be upsetting to him. There were meals to fix and medications to organize and dispense. He needed help to the bathroom and supervision in the shower. I had to clean his surgical wounds, keep his spirits up and his fever down, see that he did his breathing exercises, and answer the telephone. That alone required a secretary because the phone rang incessantly—sometimes thirty or forty times a day. We finally had to take it off the hook so I could catch an occasional nap.

I realize that caring for the ill or aging is a taxing job, but surely it is easier for those who are not emotionally involved with their patients. When caring for someone we love, we have the same physical demands as the professionals, exacerbated by mental stress. It is this kind of stress that makes our jobs so difficult. No matter how much sleep I got, I was always exhausted. I had no energy left for ordinary activities. I marvel as I see others carry on quite nicely, juggling their regular activities and caring for a family member, but I just couldn't seem to manage more than the one job.

The inevitability and the imminence of death were in the forefront of my mind. I was a walking nerve-ending, my antennae out, searching for signals and messages that might reassure me of Jim's ultimate recovery. I was in a state of readiness—watchful, wary, and ready to do battle. Fear weighed me down. The "whatifs," so aptly named in Shel Silverstein's poem, invaded my thinking.[1] "What if I spend the next forty years as a widow? What if the cancer is growing right now in the other lung? What if we're living on a pocket of radon gas that caused Jim's cancer? What if my mother dies, too, and I lose them both?" In the wee hours of the morning I came up with some doozies.

In addition to fear, there was the stress of responsibility. There were so many decisions to be made, mostly by me. I was learning I had to be an advocate, that no one else cared about my husband the way I did.

I had to work myself into a state of exhaustion before I was willing to do what I should have done in the very beginning—which was to let God do His job. I recalled a verse I had learned:

"'My grace is sufficient for you, for my strength is made perfect in weakness.' Therefore I will boast all the more gladly about my weaknesses, so that Christ's power may rest on me" (2 Cor. 12:9). I called on God to do for me what I couldn't do for myself. Because I wasn't by nature or training equipped for the job, I needed superhuman strength to take care of Jim. I leaned heavily on God for the next months, and He didn't let me down.

My days revolved around my husband and I was content to be a planet to his sun. We fell into a routine—breakfast, prayer, shower, dressing-change, arm exercises, breathing exercises, juicing (the juice had to be fresh in order to maintain the vitamins), nap, lunch, walking (a few steps around the house), nap, juicing, dinner, juicing, prayer, bed.

I did find comfort in the proscribed routine. Thankfully, I was at a place in my life where I could drop everything to deal with the crisis at hand. At least I didn't have to balance caregiving with taking care of children or an outside job. I had the perfect excuse to say "no" to every request for my participation, and I did just that.

I dug into my new job with a vengeance. I was a person obsessed, determined to do everything humanly possible to save the man I loved. I spent any spare time on the telephone or reading to find any method of treatment that might be helpful. I called people I knew who had recovered from serious illnesses. "What advice can you give me? What books can you recommend?"

I had always been a health nut so I started with holistic and natural remedies. I never considered foregoing traditional medicine, but I wanted to know what alternative treatments might be helpful. To meet my criteria, a complementary therapy had to be harmless but efficacious.

I tried several methods to build up his immune system, one of which was body-brushing. With a firm bristle brush, using small circular motions from head to foot, the epidermis is sloughed off. This was a time-consuming procedure (Jim has a big body). It probably produced only a pile of flaky skin and some minor discomfort to an already very uncomfortable patient.

I also wanted him to try visualization. You know the routine. The patient chooses some sort of scenario that is meaningful to him like Pac-men gobbling up the cancer cells or a batter slugging the offending cells out of the stadium. I am sure this works for many people, but for Jim it simply wasn't an option. Whether it was for lack of imagination or lack of motivation, I'm not sure, but he refused to participate.

We juiced—or, I should say, I juiced, he drank—for the entire six weeks between surgery and the beginning of chemo. He consumed so many carrots that his hands turned yellow. No kidding. The addition of greens to the mixture precipitated one of the three arguments we had during that entire year. He balked at the nasty tasting mixture and I flew into a rage accusing him of not doing his part to get better. When he finally started chemo, he quipped, "Bring it on, Doc. It can't be any worse than what she's been giving me at home!"

We spent more time in prayer than ever before. Our day started and ended with prayer and Bible study with Jim in the recliner where he spent most of his time, waking and sleeping. I had resumed my practice of memorizing scripture. The first one I chose was Deuteronomy 33:27. "The eternal God is your refuge, and underneath are the everlasting arms. He will drive out your enemy before you, saying, 'Destroy him!'" We clung to this promise in the days ahead as we faced the enemy that threatened us.

The next morning it became clear to me that this was the verse God meant for us to store in our hearts. An acquaintance whose husband was a good friend of Jim's called to tell me that while praying for Jim, God led her to Genesis 14:1-20. This passage is difficult reading, filled with unpronounceable names of kings and kingdoms, but the import for our situation was that we, like these Old Testament kings, were involved in a battle with the enemy—a battle that we would win with God on our side.

The call was remarkable because: (1) the woman was a very private person, one not given to making meaningless social calls; and (2) this chapter of the Bible echoed the very theme of the verse I had been led to the night before.

The next day another acquaintance phoned with a verse that came to her while she was praying for Jim. Psalm 18 is the song David sings when the Lord delivers him from the hand of all his enemies, including the formidable Saul.

I do not believe these events were coincidence; there are no coincidences with God. These women who called me were not close friends. One had never called me and the other had not called me for several years. Yet, within a forty-eight hour period, both felt moved to contact me with these verses. I saw this as an affirmation of the message in the verse we had chosen to memorize, and a confirmation that God was moving in response to our prayers.

For the second time in a matter of weeks, the Maker of the universe was speaking to me. I had heard other people say they received a message from God, but I thought either they were religious nuts, or that they were singled out by God because of their goodness. I fell into neither category—well, certainly not the second.

God *does* still speak to us today. I have proof because He spoke to me in the midst of my anguish. It was not an audible voice; nor was it preceded by lightening and thunder. But I got the message—loud and clear, and nothing will shake my belief that God sent the message just for me.

Why was I hearing from Him then when I hadn't before? I was praying and reading the Bible more. I had opened the gates of communication by placing my faith in Him and relying on His promises. I had praised Him and thanked Him, as He had told me to do through a song, and put my focus on Him and His love for us. There were countless times in those first months when I would repeat the verses I had learned.

ROAD SURVIVAL TIPS

1. Find out what to expect post-surgery.
2. Be mentally prepared for unexpected results.
3. Have someone else take the night shift, even if that means hiring a nurse.
4. Limit visitors to immediate family and then, only if they are there to help you.
5. Read "The Median Isn't the Message" by Stephen Jay Gould.[2]
6. Ignore statistics as much as you are able.
7. Listen for God's voice.

CHAPTER 3

ON THE ROAD

Toto, I have a feeling we're not in Kansas anymore.
—Dorothy Gale from L. Frank Baum's
The Wonderful Wizard of Oz

A FEW WEEKS after the surgery, our oncologist called to tell us the treatment plan. Jim would take eight to ten weeks of standard chemotherapy followed by radiation, because one of the tumors had penetrated the inner lining of the lung. No one had mentioned radiation before—another adjustment in my plans and expectations.

The doctor told us we might want to get a second opinion, while warning that a second opinion might only add to our confusion. My daughters and I had been discussing seeking another opinion, but any time we suggested it, Jim dug in his heels. He had always been a team player—loyal to his schools, his Cardinals, and his employers. He was happy with his medical team of local players—who were indeed excellent physicians—and saw no need to travel somewhere else.

I probably contributed to his insular attitude by trying to protect him from the seriousness of the disease. When anyone came to visit, Jim would tell them he was cured, that the surgeon "got it all." I cringed every time I heard him say this because what the surgeon actually said was, "We got all of the cancer *we could see.*" Almost the same words but an entirely different meaning.

We called Dr. Gary Trew, the pulmonologist who had told us a few weeks before to get our affairs in order, for his opinion. The sage advice he gave us was a turning point. "I think you should go to MD Anderson," he said to both of us on the phone. "This cancer has not behaved as anyone expected it to. Because of the way this case has unfolded, you need to go someplace where they see more of this rare cancer. Whatever the outcome, you want to be able to say you did everything possible."

We had been praying that Jim would willingly seek a second opinion, and this call was an answer to our prayers. It was not easy for him to hear what the doctor said, because for the first time he understood that the battle was far from over. He was afraid, but Dr. Trew's words provided the impetus for moving ahead. Using the internet, our daughter helped us contact MD Anderson and had the Memphis team—oncologist, internist, pulmonologist, and surgeon—send the necessary medical records to Houston. We had only been on the journey for a month and already Jim's records formed a small book.

We made an appointment with an oncologist in Houston for December 26, which meant we had to travel on Christmas day. When other families were opening gifts and drinking eggnog, we were leaving everything familiar behind to seek medical help. I didn't feel too sorry for myself—yet. The self-pity came when we arrived in a strange city, on an unusually cold winter night, for a trip that was anything but pleasurable. My spirits plummeted as we drove, in the taxi, through the deserted streets decorated with Christmas lights but void of human beings. We pulled up to a hotel that was being remodeled and was surrounded by a temporary construction wall. We couldn't figure out exactly where the office was located so the driver dumped us and our bags in what appeared to be the front of the building.

When we got to our room, one of those yet to be remodeled, I saw a scene from the 1950s. Jim only wanted to sit down; he was so exhausted he didn't care that the place looked like the Norman Bates Special. I, on the other hand, was afraid to open the shower curtain and spent a sleepless night worrying about the upcoming appointments.

The next day we went for the scans, which would be our first following the surgery. This was my initiation into the world of the waiting and I didn't much like it there. I should have been an expert because I spent much of my adult life waiting for someone. You mothers know: we wait for the baby to be born, wait at doctor appointments, wait at orthodontists, wait in carpool lines, wait at dance lessons, swim meets, soccer practices, and on and on.

Now, as a caregiver, I was learning to wait for scans to be performed, to wait for test results, to wait at bedsides, and, worst of all, to wait in the ICU. The difference was that my earlier experiences were nothing but boring. This was anything but. The world I had stepped into was fraught with anxiety and filled with doubt.

A few years earlier I developed a habit which now stood me in good stead. When one of our daughters was going through a divorce and child custody battle, I spent many hours at the courthouse waiting for her case to be heard. To pass the time in a constructive manner, I memorized scripture—something I had never done before—from a little book called *God's Promises*.[1]

Now I carried that book with me and spent time in hospitals and doctors' offices learning and reviewing scripture that I could rely on when my doubts and fears woke me in the night. Memorizing doesn't come as easy to an adult as to a child, who is more in the habit of exercising that portion of the brain. I copied the targeted verse onto a card that I carried with me in the car. At night I placed it on my bedside table so that if I awakened I could grab it for a reminder. I found it remarkably soothing to repeat the verse as I fell back to sleep.

In the afternoon we met with Dr. Adan Rios, the man who was to become an unforgettable part of our lives. Dr. Rios is a warm bear of a man with a heavy Panamanian accent who is able to deliver hard facts without robbing the patient of hope. We liked him from the very beginning. That afternoon he spent two hours with us explaining what I wanted to know from day one about the diagnosis. His philosophy of treatment for lung cancer was different from what we had heard so far.

"I believe it is critical to hit the cancer initially with every available weapon," he explained. "If we take the more conservative approach and dole the drugs out one at a time, the cancer will mutate and grow more drug-resistant. Jim's otherwise good health will allow us to be aggressive in his treatment."

We came back the next day to discuss the scan results. Dr. Rios entered the room talking, chart in hand. I loved this about him—no small talk, just straight to the point. "This is very good news. The scans confirm that the surgery did indeed remove any visible cancer. This is the beginning of a cure. The five-year survival rate for lung cancer is only about ten percent. *But*," he added, "someone is in that ten percent and it might as well be you."

At last we had a plan that made both of us feel better. We were doing something proactive to insure Jim's survival. Before he could begin treatment, Dr. Rios wanted him to have a port-a-cath surgically implanted. A port-a cath is a small device inserted in the upper chest wall to make the administration of chemotherapy drugs easier. The port, which is about the size of a thick quarter, makes a slight protrusion below the collar bone. It eliminates the need for the endless sticks and pokes and also prevents the vein damage caused by some of the more caustic drugs. Jim was reluctant to have the procedure done even though, in two months, he had already been stuck more than a ten-gallon blood donor.

Oncol Therapeutics, Dr. Rios' clinic, was relatively small as compared to some we would visit later, but the set-up was pretty much the same. The patients were in a large room circled by recliners. There were some smaller rooms reserved for patients who were unable to sit up for an extended time. Chemotherapy rooms are like refrigerators without the food. I have been told that the frigid temperatures inhibit the growth of bacteria and germs but I have my own theory: Someone is trying to kill the patients before they succumb to the disease. The victims recline in their paradoxically named easy chairs, most of them sleeping, while the various drugs drip into their veins.

We arrived at the oncology clinic early in the morning with much trepidation because we had heard the horror stories about chemo. Before we began, the technician gave us literature from the drug manufacturers warning of all the possible side effects, some of which were permanent or even fatal. Like smokers reading the warnings on the cigarette packages, believing that the warnings didn't apply to us, we forged right ahead. What alternative did we have? We believed that without treatment he would die anyway.

I have no doubt that someday our descendants will think of chemotherapy in the same way we think of leeches. I can imagine a conversation among our great-great grandchildren. "You can't mean that doctors actually put these toxic drugs into the bloodstreams of human beings. How barbaric! Didn't the stuff kill some of them?" (Yes, actually it did.)

In reading *The Secret History of the War on Cancer*[2] I learned about the development of chemotherapeutic agents. During World War I, soldiers who had been exposed to mustard gas and managed to survive were found to have a dramatic decrease in their white blood counts. Knowing that leukemia was a disease causing an increase in the number of white blood cells, researchers proposed that a poison like mustard gas might reverse these blood counts in cancer patients. The problem was the same one we face today—how to kill the bad cells before killing the host.

Most certainly the chemotherapy drugs have been refined since mustard gas, but the side effects are not much different from those exhibited by the unfortunate victims of World War I—nausea, nerve damage, loss of hair, breathing difficulty, and pain. I watched as my husband experienced all of these and more.

There is a world of difference between reading about possible side effects and experiencing those side effects. We had been warned about the chemo drugs, but I didn't know about the additional drugs given to counteract the effects of the chemo. Each therapeutic infusion is preceded by a cocktail of anti-nausea medication, Benadryl, and steroids. Believe me, the pre-infusion is bad enough. One drug stimulates the patient while another relaxes him. Each time Jim received this mixture he would doze while his body intermittently jerked him awake in response to the Decadron (a multi-purpose steroid used to prevent allergic reaction, nausea, and treat certain cancers). As I watched the poison drip into his body, I prayed, "God, please guide this drug to the cancer cells and protect the healthy cells." I sat by helplessly watching for some kind of severe reaction that the nurses or doctors might miss.

No one told us the pre-infusion isn't always enough to avert the nausea, that frequently additional medication is necessary post-treatment. The first night he awoke with violent vomiting and nausea. We were understandably frightened because we had heard that the effects of the treatments were cumulative. "How will he ever make it through if it gets worse than this?" I thought.

Thankfully, through trial and error we found a solution. When Jim came home from a session, he took Phenergan (which was allowed for break-through nausea) before bed. The next morning, sick or not, he would take a strong anti-nausea med. This formula seemed to work for him. He sometimes had mild nausea, but never like the first time. Once is enough. For us, the trick with nausea was to be proactive, just as with pain. Never let the process get started. We have shared this simple finding with many others who also report success.

Many of the drugs a cancer patient takes are to curb the side-effects of the actual cancer fighting agents. Three times a week I would inject Jim in the abdomen with a drug intended to bolster the production of red blood cells in the bone marrow. Once a week I gave him a shot in the thigh for the production of white blood cells. As these drugs did their work, he experienced severe pain in his legs, requiring yet another drug to combat pain.

Formation of blood clots occurs in about ten percent of chemotherapy patients. Once again, we fell into that small percentage when Jim formed a blood clot in his right shoulder near the area of the port. When he awakened with his left arm swollen to nearly twice the size of the right, we immediately rushed to the cancer clinic. (Had I not been at home, he would not have recognized how serious this symptom was. This reinforced the belief—right or wrong—

that I needed to stay with him all the time.) A blood clot can be fatal if it moves to the lungs. After determining the exact location of the clot, they sent him home on high dosages of Coumadin and Fragmin (blood-thinning drugs). Now I would be giving him two additional shots in the stomach daily. My medical education was progressing.

We had a rough couple of weeks. The blood clot required daily trips to The West Clinic for monitoring. It was responding to the medication—but slowly. The side effects of the chemo, not surprisingly, were cumulative. Jim felt like he had the flu, complete with body aches, nausea, tremendous fatigue, and painful ulcers covering his mouth. Pain in his chest and back, normal after thoracic surgery, still scared me. When he wasn't at the clinic, he slept. In fact, when he was at the clinic he slept. He seldom complained and never whined, but it was hard for me to watch him suffer.

He had lost his hair, of course, but that didn't really bother either of us. It did make me sad to see his scarred body. Jim always had a beautiful body, speaking in an aesthetic sense. He was an Illinois farm boy, of German descent, tall and "stout" as his Nana said. He also had rosy cheeks and skin that would put the Breck girl to shame. Now he had the large scar from the thoracotomy circling the left side of his chest and back, scars from the drainage tubes on his side, the scar from the port on his chest, and numerous bruises from injections on his stomach, thighs, and arms.

Jim was understandably moody. Part of this was a result of the Decadron he took in the pre-infusion and orally for several days afterward. He was agitated and excitable when he was on the drug and depressed as he came off. Just about the time his mood leveled, the time came to start another round.

While in Houston, on days when Jim didn't receive treatment, we tried to get out for a change of scenery. We took a few trips to the bookstore where I would pour over any book about cancer while he would sit in a comfortable chair and read a novel. It was on one of these expeditions to Barnes and Noble that we had our second major argument.

Jim had absolutely no interest in reading about cancer, nor did he want to hear me talk about it. He was content to have me do the research, bring it to him on a platter, and let him pick and choose whichever morsels he deemed worthy. When I presented him with my latest finding, another book about visualization as a technique for fighting cancer, he turned his nose up and refused to take even a "scout's bite." Disappointed because he wouldn't so much as consider the merits of the idea (one which I was convinced would lead to a rapid, painless cure), I spun on my heel and said, "We might as well go back to the hotel, since I appear to be wasting my time."

Not one to let a good fight die, when we got into the shuttle, still seething, I said, "You know, I can't spoon-feed you. It does no good for me to find information if you won't put it to use. I can visualize 'til the cows come home and it won't do a thing for your body. I am sick of trying to find ways to help you when you won't help yourself. From here on out, you're on your own."

I stared out the window, holding back tears, as we rode in silence back to the hotel. The outburst was no more than an explosion of pent up feelings. I never gave up on him—and he never tried visualization.

TIPS FOR THE ROAD

1. Consider getting a second opinion from a comprehensive cancer center.
2. Memorize scripture.
3. At every chemotherapy session, check to see that the patient is receiving the correct drugs.
4. Learn about the drugs your loved one will take.
5. Dress warmly for test facilities, treatment centers, and hospitals.
6. Be prepared for mood swings—yours and the patient's.

CHAPTER 4

THE ROAD TO THE CRAZY HOUSE

No one ever told me that grief felt so like fear.
—C.S. Lewis

THERE WERE TIMES I thought the road we were on would lead straight to the crazy house. I was hanging tenuously to my seat, but knew the next bump might throw me from the car.

Jim was suffering mood swings from Decadron; I'm not sure what my excuse was. Although I didn't recognize it, I suppose I was mildly depressed. I had the classic symptoms—fatigue, lack of motivation, and a general malaise.

Depression frequently accompanies a cancer diagnosis for both patient and caregiver. On the advice of our daughter Nicole, a clinical psychologist, and with the approval of Jim's doctors, we started taking an antidepressant. Neither of us had taken an antidepressant before but we were open to the suggestion. Many Christians see these drugs as unnecessary crutches used by those who are weak in their faith. I never shared this opinion, so taking them did not present a conflict for me. Depression is a real physiological imbalance that can sometimes be alleviated by psycho-pharmaceuticals.

Five years after Jim's original diagnosis, I came across an article in *Cure* magazine about the emotional struggles of the caregiver. Had I read the article earlier, I might have realized that many people who get a poor diagnosis experience depression and grief. I thought I was guilty of self-pity, but come to find out, psychologists have given this kind of emotional upheaval a name—anticipatory grief. When the patient's prognosis is poor, the caregiver anticipates the death and experiences the same emotions that accompany the death of a loved one. Thoughts like, "What will happen to me?" and "How will I manage alone?" are not self-centered, but rather, appropriate reactions in the situation.[1]

Even if the disease doesn't end in death, there is still loss—loss of dreams, loss of health, loss of identity, loss of shared participation in physical activities, loss of occupation. Frequently, there is loss of physical intimacy as treatment progresses. I thought when Jim retired we would travel, play tennis, and watch our grandchildren grow up. Now I had to re-evaluate my plans.

I shouldn't have been surprised to find myself grieving, but I was not prepared for the feelings I had. The patient and spouse are likely to go through the now widely recognized stages outlined by Elisabeth Kubler-Ross in her 1969 book *On Death and Dying*. She applied these stages to any kind of catastrophic event, but they are associated more often with death. I was familiar with her theory but didn't think it applied to me as a caregiver whose spouse was very much alive.

According to Kubler-Ross there are five stages: denial, anger, bargaining, depression, and acceptance. The stages might not be in that order, nor does everyone experience all of them, but she said a grieving person will always experience at least two.[2]

The denial and anger stages are defense mechanisms that buy time, allowing one to adjust to the shock of diagnosis. I see the denial stage as a gift from God, a chance to marshal forces and strength before the full realization hits. My ignorance kept me from recognizing the wide impact of a lung cancer diagnosis. When I was ready, God revealed the path ahead, one step at a time.

Jim probably exhibited more of the classic denial symptoms than I did. During our first trip to Houston, we were talking with another cancer patient in the waiting room. He was a ten-year prostate cancer survivor who attributed part of his longevity to the supplement COQ_{10}. After he left, I turned to Jim and said, "That might be something we should try. I've read some studies about the benefits."

His response left me jaw-gaping: "It might be good for that guy—but he has cancer," he said with all sincerity. Talk about denial. No doubt this mechanism protected him at a time when he was overwhelmed by other emotions, but I had to fight the need to set him straight. I wanted someone else to be as afraid as I was.

Neither Jim nor I went through the anger stage, but our daughters did. Why should their dad, who had taken such good care of himself, get lung cancer, while so many chain-smoking, overweight slackers remained healthy? Their feelings were obvious in the glares directed toward anyone who dared to light up a cigarette in their presence. Though the smokers weren't responsible for Jim's cancer, they were a safer object of their wrath than God.

Anger against God is never justifiable, but it is understandable. Many of God's faithful went through periods of anger. Job, in the midst of his suffering, beseeched God, "Do not condemn me, but tell me what charges you have against me. Does it please you to oppress me, to spurn the work of you hands, while you smile on the schemes of the wicked?" (Job 10:2-3).

Jeremiah, unappreciated and forsaken by the people he was trying to save, cursed the day he was born and cried out to God asking why he, who had been obedient and faithful, should suffer so. "I never sat in the company of revelers, never made merry with them; I sat alone because your hand was on me and you had filled me with indignation. Why is my pain unending and my wound grievous and incurable? Will you be to me like a deceptive brook, like a spring that fails?" (Jer. 15:17-18). The cancer patient might ask God these same things. "What I have I done to deserve this suffering? Why are you not listening to me? Why won't you heal me?"

I didn't do much bargaining with God but I do remember praying that if Jim could just make it for five years, I would be happy. Of course, now that five years have come and gone, I wish I had asked for twenty. Jim didn't bargain but he offered specific prayers: "Let me live to see the birth of this new grandchild. Let me fulfill my obligation as deacon chairman." I don't know that he promised anything in return for the granting of those petitions, so that might not qualify as bargaining.

Many caregivers report fear, anxiety, and guilt. While not specifically included in Kubler-Ross's five stages, they fall under the umbrella of depression. Whether or not they were recognized, all were problems for me.

I experienced fear and anxiety because of my lack of control. The less control I had over cancer, the more I craved control over other aspects of my life. I couldn't make plans because life kept interfering with them. I had to relinquish control daily—sometimes more frequently—putting myself in the hands of my Creator. This was not easy for me. I'd give a little, then take it back. Every move toward acceptance was countered by a backward move toward fear.

I tried to analyze the fear, thinking that if I could understand it I could conquer it. Facing the death of a spouse is more difficult than facing your own death. The thought of watching Jim suffer, maybe die, and spending whatever time I had left on earth without him was unbearable. I knew that God promises to give comfort to the brokenhearted, to give us strength when we have none, to lift us from the deepest pit, and He had certainly done that for me. But if my worst fears were realized, would my grief be so big that God couldn't give me the peace that passes understanding?

I knew that God is all powerful and that He never breaks His promises. But what if I was too weak? The weaker we are, the better able He is to show His mighty power, for His "power is made perfect in weakness. Therefore I will boast all the more gladly about my weaknesses, so that Christ's power may rest on me" (2 Cor. 12:9). So what was I afraid of? That my faith wouldn't be great enough? Or, the most terrible thing I could imagine, that I would lose my faith completely? Maybe I would be like Job's wife instead of Job and curse God when things didn't go my way. *What if I became a bitter old lady unable to find joy in anything? Could God really provide me with the strength I needed, or would He need a little better raw material to work with?*

At one of our recent support group meetings, one of the ladies, newly diagnosed with breast cancer said, "I just don't know how to do this. I'm afraid I won't be good at it. The rest of you are so strong."

"There is no right or wrong way to make a journey of this kind," I explained to her. "Each of us reacts differently depending on our personality, emotional makeup, and our previous experience." Sometimes we are our harshest critics. It does no good to judge ourselves or others.

In the beginning, I didn't think I had a right to my feelings because I wasn't the one who was sick. But I had begun to see his illness as my own. I spoke of *our* appointments, *our* oncologists, *our* scans, and *our* journey. The incorrect use of the plural, inclusive pronouns was an indication of the enmeshment that had occurred. I had no life of my own and I didn't really care. I wasn't sure if my identification with my husband was a good thing as in "two becoming one," joined together by the marriage vows, or an unhealthy co-dependency which called for the intervention of a psychiatrist.

I was exhausted but I felt guilty if I complained. Actually, I didn't complain, but felt guilty because I felt like complaining! I berated myself. *Stop this self-pity. You should be able to handle this. What kind of wimp are you? Where is your faith?*

To complicate matters, my mother, who had been in the hospital recovering from a broken hip, was ready to come home. I was torn between her needs and Jim's. She didn't want or expect me to be with her, but I hated for her to be alone. I was being stretched like an exercise band—the large blue one.

I was taking the antidepressant, but quite frankly, I was a nervous wreck. I made an appointment with a psychologist in hopes that she might help me handle my emotions and live with the uncertainty and the transitions I was making. She didn't really tell me anything that helped, so I only saw her once. Had I known then about the stages of grief, I would have chosen a counselor who specialized in that area, but I didn't even understand that I was grieving. I thought it was premature at that early date, and somehow admitting those feelings seemed disloyal to Jim. I probably should have looked for another counselor, but I didn't have the time or energy.

God had heard my cries during the first few weeks after Jim's diagnosis and miraculously, true to His Word, lifted me up and held me in the palm of His hand. But that situation, as awful as it was, wasn't hopeless. I got what I wanted—Jim was alive and with me, and feeling relatively well. What if the outcome had been otherwise? Would I have been obedient to God, offered Him thanks in the midst of the trial, praised Him with song and witness? In the words of Hamlet, "Aye, there's the rub."

The road to acceptance would take me on some interesting detours before the final destination.

How to Avoid the Crazy House

1. Consider an antidepressant.
2. Seek professional counseling.
3. Allow yourself to grieve.
4. Don't waste energy on guilt.
5. Admit your feelings—to yourself and others.

CHAPTER 5

A DETOUR—
EXPLORING MY FAITH

We don't receive wisdom; we must discover it for ourselves after a journey that no one can take for us or spare us.

—Marcel Proust

PEOPLE RESPOND IN different ways to the diagnosis of a life-threatening disease. Some pretend the lion is not in the room—until he bites off their head. Many experience a psychological and spiritual crisis in which they question the meaning of life and death. Others accept peacefully what is happening as God's will, trusting fully that God will heal them on earth or at the moment of death.

Jim was one of the latter. Early in his illness he would infuriate our daughters by proclaiming he was completely at peace. *Was he in denial? Didn't he realize how poor his prognosis was? Did he understand that his long term survival was unlikely?*

He might have been at peace, but the rest of us were far from it. Now, after talking with many other patients and their families, I realize the response of the patient is very different from that of the caregiver. If the patient is a Christian he might readily accept the possibility of his death, knowing he is promised eternity in the presence of a loving God. But what about those left behind?

I, for one, did not look forward to spending the next thirty years as a widow waiting to be reunited with my husband in Paradise. He might be floating on a cloud in heavenly bliss, but I would be pining away in an empty house listening for things that go bump in the night.

Never very good at sticking my head in the sand, I became a part of the group that seeks answers to life's basic questions. (In the 1970s, we called this existential angst.) The only way I could get through the journey was to face the grim reaper head on and learn more about him. To find my peace, I had to accept the possibility of Jim's death, and then pray for the miracle that would prevent it.

I've sometimes envied those who can live in a state of denial, seemingly oblivious to anything that might shake their false sense of security. In John Piper's "Don't Waste Your Cancer,"[1] he writes that you will waste your cancer if you don't face your death and recognize your mortality. We are all terminal. One of the blessings of cancer is that we know that our stay on earth is temporary, so we carefully consider what comes next.

Sigmund Freud wrote in his essay "Thoughts for the Time on War and Death," "Would it not be better to give death the place in reality and in our thoughts which it so deserves and to give a little more prominence to the unconscious attitude towards death which we hitherto so carefully repressed. We remember the old saying: *Si vis pacem, para bellum*. If you desire peace, prepare for war. It would be timely to thus paraphrase it: *Si vis vitam, para mortem*. If you would endure life, be prepared for death."[2] Life can't be your friend when death is your enemy.

Not everyone finds it necessary to set out on this quest for faith assurance. God made us individuals—some require proof, others are happy to accept information from authority. The difference is not level of intelligence. My own mother, one of the smartest people I've known, never questioned her beliefs. But I was different; I needed answers.

I had no doubts about the existence of God, but what about Jesus? Who was He? Did He really rise from the dead? What happens when we die? Did I believe the Apostles' Creed that I had been taught as a child?

"I believe in God, the Father Almighty,
the Creator of heaven and earth,
and in Jesus Christ, His only Son, our Lord:
Who was conceived of the Holy Spirit,
born of the Virgin Mary, suffered under Pontius Pilate,
was crucified, died, and was buried. He descended into hell.
The third day He arose again from the dead. He ascended into heaven and sits at the right hand of God the Father Almighty,

whence He shall come to judge the living and the dead. I believe in the Holy Spirit, the holy Christian church, the communion of saints, the forgiveness of sins, the resurrection of the body, and life everlasting."

I couldn't rely on God's promises and find comfort in His word if I didn't truly believe the basic tenets of Christianity. Did I believe because I was afraid not to when the alternative is so bleak? Or were the beliefs I clung to real?

I confessed my doubts to God and asked Him to give me wisdom in my search. God gave us brains and expects us to use them. He doesn't mind when we question the Bible. In the book of Mark, when a man brings his son to Jesus for healing, Jesus tells him He is able to do anything for those who believe. "Immediately the boy's father exclaimed, 'I do believe; help me overcome my unbelief!'" (Mark 9:24). Jesus healed the boy—presumably securing the father's belief.

I took time out of my cancer research and delved into the Bible and books by great thinkers on the topics of death and resurrection. I started with a book I read a few years before, *The Case for Christ*, by Lee Strobel. Strobel, a Yale-educated legal-affairs journalist who considered himself an atheist, married a woman who became a Christian. To understand what was happening to his wife, he set out on a spiritual quest for the truth about Jesus Christ.[3]

During his two year search he interviewed leading scholars and religious authorities about the historical evidence for the existence of Christ. Though he was skeptical, the results of his research convinced him that Jesus was indeed the son of God.

I read *Mere Christianity* by C.S. Lewis[4], *God: The Evidence* by Patrick Glynn[5], *The Language of God* by Francis S. Collins[6], and several other authors whose faith was integral to their lives and writings. I was reassured to know that men and women much smarter than I believed the things I wanted to believe.

I found it easier to believe and trust God when I looked behind and realized He had led me on the right path all throughout my life. When I gave thanks to God as He told me to do in the first week of our journey, I was recalling the ways in which He had blessed us and kept His promises to us. If we are in the habit of thanking and praising God, recalling His past faithfulness is not difficult.

In his book *When Your Doctor Has Bad News,* Dr. Al Weir writes about how an Albanian pastor he met on a mission trip explained his faith. "Faith is moving through life as if we were rowing a boat to our destination, and we are watching for direction from our Pilot, who can see clearly from his position standing in the rear of the boat. As he tells us to pull harder on the right oar or harder on the left, we continue to move in the direction he chooses. Then as we see our lives moving past us, we realize his direction was true, and we gain confidence that he will take us where we wish to be."[7] When I have doubts, I find it helpful to look back at the times God has revealed His presence to me.

After my research, although I was *reasonably* convinced of the truth of the Bible, I still had to make a leap of *faith.* There are many mysteries in the Bible that we, with our limited brains, will never understand. "Now faith is being sure of what we hope for and certain of what we do not see"

(Heb. 11:1). No matter how much proof you are presented, in the final analysis you must make a choice.

Faith requires action on our part. We choose to obey, choose to be thankful, and choose to believe. Dr. Weir writes about the relationship between faith, trust, obedience, and answered prayer. "God has developed a pipeline for his power with a valve at our end that must be opened. Faith is the knob that opens the pipeline of God's power."[8]

God commands us to praise Him and thank Him in the midst of our suffering or trials. When we do this, even though we don't "feel" like doing it, we open a channel that allows Him to work in our lives. I know that sounds mystical, certainly supernatural, because it is. We don't receive the blessings God has for us until we relinquish our imagined control to Him. In doing that we take off His handcuffs so that He can give us all He wants us to have.

A few years ago, after we had received more bad news about Jim's cancer, our daughter sent us these thoughts about her own faith walk: "Some people believe Christianity is a crutch for the emotionally weak. I disagree. True faith requires more strength than do intellectualization and reason. Unfortunately the word 'faith' sounds passive—like something that accompanies spirituality, a buy-one-get-one-free. But 'faith' should be a verb because it is a constant activity requiring prayer and worship. The process is somewhat paradoxical because 'faithing' is the hardest thing I've ever done, but when I get there I have the easiest feeling I've ever had. Everything makes sense and I understand my purpose. Without true faith, the best we can hope for is a numbing of emotional pain. And I don't think that's what a relationship with God is all about. I don't want to go through life in an analgesic state. I want to experience life as He has designed it for me. The only way to do this is through an active, relinquishing 'faithing.'"

Christ confronted Peter and asked, "Who do you say I am?" The answer to that question is the crux of Christianity. I chose to take the leap of faith and believe that Jesus Christ is the Son of God, who came to earth, was crucified, and rose from the dead. Secure in that belief, I could move on to the question that precipitated my search. If Jesus was the resurrected Son of God, what happens to *us* when *we* die?

By the time we reach middle-age, most of us have lived through the death of a loved one. If we are lucky, those deaths came in a natural order—the death of a pet, the death of grandparents, great-aunts or uncles, and, for many of us, the death of a parent. Many have experienced deaths outside the natural order and lost a parent, sibling, or child early in life. When those losses occur, we learn something about the process of death and how to handle sorrow and grief. For me, none of those experiences caused me to face my own mortality as did the illness of my husband.

Some of you have probably stopped reading and others are reading with reservation, because death is not a topic we are fond of discussing. Death has been sanitized, hospitalized, and institutionalized so that members of our generation have seen less of it than our parents and grandparents did. People used to die at home surrounded by children and loved ones. Now we are shielded from this experience, depriving us of the opportunity to view death as a natural, inevitable part of life.

God has given us such a beautiful earth to enjoy. Because of my human limitations, I am unable to grasp that there is a place more beautiful. Sitting at the feet of Jesus, singing praises with the saints, would be enjoyable for an hour or two, but I'm afraid this type-A, slightly ADHD person, would soon be bored. As a resident of the heavenly kingdom, will I miss a good tennis game on a crisp autumn afternoon when every ball magically hits the mark? What could be better than a Saturday night with Jim in front of the TV watching 24 and eating a gooey cheese pizza? Will I long for a winter night snugly cocooned in my Sterns and Foster with a thick novel? What about watching the winter cardinals eating from our feeder or scratching my fat cat's chin as he curls up on my lap? Is what God has in store better than all of this?

I must admit I don't yearn for the heavenly experience the way I expect others might. I have a foot like lead mired in the business of this world, even though my eyes are on the heavenly prize. But in the midst of cancer God showed me that life on this earth is fleeting; every one of us is terminal. Day by day we age and die. The beauty is that, as our bodies die, we also die to self and become more like Jesus. For the transformation to be complete, we have to leave the shell of our bodies in order to be resurrected and live with Him. "Therefore we do not lose heart. Though outwardly we are wasting away, yet inwardly we are being renewed day by day. So we fix our eyes not on what is seen, but on what is unseen. For what is seen is temporary, but what is unseen is eternal" (2 Cor. 4:16, 18).

The "faithing" detour affirmed my belief in the resurrection of Jesus Christ. I believe He is the Son of God who came to earth in human form, died on the cross, and rose again from the dead. Because I can say this with conviction, death "loses its sting." Death has been conquered and is not, of itself, to be feared. "Jesus said to her, 'I am the resurrection and the life. He who believes in me will live, even though he dies; and whoever lives and believes in me will never die. Do you believe this?'" (John 11:25-26). For believers, "There is no death, though eyes grow dim."[9]

How can this be? It is another of those mysteries beyond human comprehension. But fortunately there are times when God gives us glimpses of the eternal so we can know these things are true. I have had many of these glimpses on the cancer journey. To know your enemy is good advice, and in attempting to do that, I came to see that death is not the enemy; cancer is the enemy and a formidable foe it is.

Now when fear comes, I remind myself:

1. I am not a citizen of the earth but rather a citizen of a heavenly kingdom.
2. All of us are here for a very short time as ambassadors for our King.
3. Death is not an end but a return to the place we really belong.

DIRECTIONS FOR THE DETOUR

1. If you are having doubts, go to God in prayer and ask Him to increase your faith.
2. Study your Bible.
3. Read the faith stories of other Christians.
4. Look back in gratitude at what God has done.
5. Choose to believe.
6. Choose to obey.

CHAPTER 6

FUEL FOR BODY AND SPIRIT— GOD'S PROVISIONS

Then Jacob made a vow, saying, "If God will be with me and will watch over me on this journey I am taking and will give me food to eat and clothes to wear so that I return safely to my father's house, then the Lord will be my God and this stone that I have set up as a pillar will be God's house, and of all that you give me I will give you a tenth."
—Genesis 28:20-22 NIV

I F JESUS IS the Son of God, able to resurrect the dead, then healing the sick should present no problem for Him. Yet, I cannot now, nor have I ever been able to, say with conviction that I know God will heal a particular person—on this earth—of whatever affliction he might have.

I believe God will ultimately heal us at the moment of death, but that is not the assurance most people want. When

I pray with other caregivers, they are praying for healing of the physical body in the present time—not the healing that comes with death.

In a recent sermon, Dr. Ernie Frey said, "God meets us at our tombs, not just where we are resurrected. He shows up at the messes in our lives and heals." Dr. Frey was referring to the raising of Lazarus from the dead. Jesus came to the aid of Mary and Martha, His friends, and met them at the tomb, their place of need—on earth.

God is still in the miracle business just as he was in the time of Lazarus. By definition, a miracle occurs when God intervenes and the outcome that one would expect in the realm of natural law is changed. The question for me comes in knowing when God will intervene, when He will perform a miracle.

I know He is able, but is He willing? Why doesn't He heal everyone? Is healing directly proportional to the faith of those praying? What about the number of people praying? Is God more likely to grant the miracle if a multitude of people are beseeching Him? How does prayer work? What good does it do to pray if God's mind is already made up? Why do some people get the answers they want to their prayers while others don't?

We are told: "The prayer of a righteous man is powerful and effective" (James 5:16). And "Again, I tell you that if two of you on earth agree about anything you ask for, it will be done for you by my Father in heaven. For where two or three come together in my name, there am I with them" (Matt. 18:19-20).

Yet, I have seen many good, devout Christians die, in spite of heartfelt prayers by a bastion of the faithful. And I have seen others, perhaps less religious, get the miracle they prayed for, outliving a dire prognosis. Experience has shown me that healing has nothing to do with the amount of faith or the righteousness of the one being prayed for.

How, then, does prayer work?

I sought scientific explanations. Physicists have known for many years that time is relative and that matter and energy are connected. As we learn more about the universe, the impossible becomes explicable. Quantum theory in physics now shows us that particles far removed from each other, which came from the same source of energy, can "communicate" across great distances.[1] If we are created of the same matter as the Creator, is it such a stretch that we are able somehow to connect with Him?

Physicists have also proven that time is relative.[2] I've always known that our concept of time is limited, while to God time is meaningless. "For a thousand years in your sight are like a day that has just gone by" (Ps. 90:4). "With the Lord a day is like a thousand years, and a thousand years are like a day" (2 Pet. 3:8). As we learn more about our world we see that the conflicts between science and religion are not so great.

Before I knew Jesus personally, I thought praying was a psychological exercise, beneficial in sorting out problems and marshalling my energy toward a desired goal. I did not consider prayer a two-way conversation with the almighty God. Nor did I believe that through prayer I was connecting to the source of all power. I considered myself a believer, but I misunderstood the process of prayer. I prayed, but depended on my own ability for strength and accomplishment. With this view of prayer, it is not surprising that I didn't believe others could pray effectively for me. Until I had the indwelling Holy Spirit, I was not able to have intimacy with God or begin to understand anything about Him.

At the time of Jim's diagnosis we belonged to a megachurch. Jim had a position of leadership, giving us a built-in base of prayer warriors. From the day we made our needs known, people across the country began praying for Jim. As months passed, we met people from different churches and even different cities who had been praying for us, although we were unaware.

In the hospital, when I was too distraught to pray myself, friends took up the slack and petitioned God on our behalf. When Jim was in a drug-induced sleep, others were praying for him. When I awakened at night, I was greatly comforted to know someone was praying for us. Although I didn't understand intercessory prayer, I began to realize the value. I resolved never again to say, "I'll pray for you," unless I fully intended to follow through. And as for those who promised to "think good thoughts,"—I appreciated the sentiment, but I had learned that thoughts alone lack the effectiveness of prayer, which is directed to the original power source. Positive thoughts can help the "thinker" but not so much the person being "thought of."

I had never experienced prayer like this on my behalf. Crises earlier in my life involved the kind of family secrets I wasn't eager to share. I shoved them in the closet, hoping the skeletons wouldn't be discovered until years after I was gone. Because this particular crisis involved no stigma, imagined or real, I shared it with a multitude of people who were then able and willing to support us in a variety of ways.

Before we can receive the blessing of the prayers of those interceding for us, we have to humble ourselves and let our needs be known. In past times, pride kept me from admitting my need for help. Whether God is affected by the number of people praying is not the important consideration. He is moved by our willingness to depend on the body of believers demonstrating faith in Him.

Cancer is a great leveler. I think people saw us as a perfect family—healthy, successful, and free from problems. Because I had been brought up to not air my dirty laundry in public, people perceived me as stand-offish. To make matters worse, I was an introvert who didn't need large groups of friends for self-fulfillment. But after cancer I saw that no man is an island. I had to depend on others for help and support. Over the years I had missed countless blessings because I was unwilling to make myself vulnerable.

Our problems made us more approachable. As a result we were able to observe the beauty of the church body at work. I am not talking about an individual church (although the church we were attending at that time provided a large portion of our help), but rather the church in the larger sense—the body of believers in Christ. Dr. Ernie Frey said in his sermon on Lazarus: "Just as Martha and Mary removed the grave clothes of Lazarus, enabling him to walk freely, the modern Church should help remove the grave clothes of those in need of help."

The Church removed our grave clothes and helped us, not only through prayer but in more tangible ways. When we came home after Jim's surgery in November, our Sunday school class and my Bible study provided meals for two months. Another friend did my grocery shopping. Neighbors took out the garbage and ran errands for us. One weekend I looked outside and saw a family—people I didn't know—raking the leaves in our yard.

We received hundreds of calls and cards from friends and acquaintances. One of the ministers at our church called regularly to check just on *me*—a kindness I have never forgotten. When we were out of town for treatment, away from family and friends for weeks, our class sent us a care package, filled with all sorts of snacks and little gifts to lift our spirits. My tennis team sent me a box of books—their favorite reads. At Christmas, a group of carolers, knowing Jim was house-bound, came to the door bringing the message of the birth of the Savior. Cancer put us on the receiving end of many acts of kindness.

I wish I could tell you that my quest gave me answers to all of my questions. I cannot. I doubt that man will ever be able to explain the way God works, the mysteries of the universe, or the way in which we can converse with the creator. "'For my thoughts are not your thoughts, neither are your ways my ways,' declares the Lord" (Isa. 55:8). During our journey, I didn't find all the answers to life's mysteries but I did learn more about the character of God. As I came to know Him better, I understood more of the "whys" if not the "hows."

As I learned about God, my insatiable need to know the future was fading. I was content to trust the driver to equip me for the journey. Exactly how He accomplished that didn't matter. I still don't understand how prayer works, but I know it does. I still don't understand how God heals, but I know He does. I still don't understand much of God's activity, but I know that, just as He did with Martha and Mary, He met me where I was and provided all that I needed, at exactly the right time.

He didn't always answer my prayers the way I wanted; He didn't always answer in my time frame. But just as He provided manna for the Israelites each day, He provided my daily bread. I had to learn not to look into the future but accept what He gave me in the present. The Israelites might have preferred steak, but the manna was sufficient for their needs.

I was amazed at how God met our financial needs during this time—first with the disability insurance. Jim's company had a disability policy on all of the employees. In addition to this standard policy, Jim had taken out his own policy early in his career—an unusual move because most of the people in his industry don't see the need for supplemental insurance. Jim had actually forgotten about it until we started receiving a check! I wasn't aware of either of the policies, which isn't surprising considering my ignorance of all financial matters.

Isn't it astonishing that God, knowing Jim would have cancer, guided him to take out this insurance, years before he would need it? Not only did we receive the unexpected income, we found the benefits were based on his salary two years earlier—before the market made the downward slide resulting in a significant cut in his paycheck.

When we were seeking a second opinion, Jim, forever practical, asked me to check with MD Anderson and Oncol Therapeutics (the facility Dr. Rios opened when he left MD Anderson) to be sure they accepted our insurance carrier. MD Anderson did; Oncol Therapeutics did not. "I'm not going anywhere if they don't accept our insurance," Jim stated flatly.

"I don't care what it costs," was my naive reply. "You have to go where you can get the best care." Obviously, I had no idea about the cost of cancer treatment. I just figured that if you were sick and needed treatment someone had to provide it.

When we decided to go to Dr. Rios for our second opinion, Jim suggested I call again to check about the insurance, although they had told us a month earlier they would not accept ours. I called the office and explained our situation. The assistant said, "Hang on a minute. Let me check something." In a few minutes she came back to the phone. "You're in luck. We began accepting United Health Care on November 1."

Luck? I don't think so. On November 1, Jim had the appointment for the routine physical that would mark the beginning of this journey. The perfect timing of the insurance coverage was another indication that God was in control and had been from the very beginning.

I don't know why He provided for us the way He did when others face tremendous financial hardship during their journeys. Perhaps I was seeing the law of the harvest at work. The principle: You reap what you sow; you reap more than you sow; you reap in good time, later than you sow. "Remember this: Whoever sows sparingly will also reap sparingly, and whoever sows generously will also reap generously. Each man should give what he has decided in his heart to give, not reluctantly or under compulsion, for God loves a cheerful giver. And God is able to make all grace abound to you, so that in all things at all times, having all that you need, you will abound in every good work" (2 Cor. 9:6-8).

Early in the journey, Jim set the tone for our attitude about money. On Saturday morning, the day after we received the diagnosis, I woke up and found him already in the kitchen sitting by the fire. He said, "I am going to the bank on Monday to make a withdrawal."

We had made a pledge to the church building fund, part due in December and the remainder in February. Jim was a financial planner and our income had already been cut in half over the two previous years because of the poor performance of the stock market following 9/11. Now we were faced with even more uncertainty, knowing he would be out of work for a month or more, in a business in which he was compensated strictly in commissions.

Jim made the decision to step out in faith, to honor our commitment, and to trust God to provide. I certainly respected his decision, but I'm not so sure I would have done the same without his leading. For maybe the first time ever, I was being asked to give sacrificially. Any other time we made a pledge, I left the amount up to Jim since he handled all the finances. I trusted him and gave very little thought to how it would affect me. Now I gave serious consideration to honoring the obligation, knowing we might need the money in the days ahead.

Because of Jim's obedience in this financial matter, God blessed him by providing for him in countless ways throughout the course of his illness. This law is not a magic formula for prosperity. I know God doesn't promise remuneration to everyone who tithes or gives to the church. What God honors is the attitude of cheerful sharing while depending on Him to meet our needs. He provides what we need when we need it, although the provision may come in different ways.

Because of God's love for us, demonstrated in the sacrifice of his Son, He wants communion with us. Our prayers are pleasing to Him. He does not promise to heal us; He does promise to provide and sustain us in times of trouble. God meets us at our place of pain and provides what we need.

PACKING YOUR BAGS

1. Ask for prayer.
2. Pray (converse with God) consistently.
3. Accept help.
4. Give back to God what belongs to God.
5. Know what your benefits are—disability, Social Security, and insurance.

CHAPTER 7

STREAMS IN THE DESERT

*Nothing softens a journey so pleasantly as an
account of misfortunes at which the hearer is
permitted to laugh.*

—Quentin Crisp

I DIDN'T ASK for cancer, but I'm glad I had it." Only
someone who has been through a serious illness while
leaning on the Lord can understand how anyone in his
right mind can make that statement. Yet, both Jim and I
have found the good that comes with cancer outweighs the
pain and suffering. God has hidden nuggets of blessings in
the trials of our lives.

Can Christians find joy when their lives are shattered?
Or is the promise of joy fulfilled only when we get to
heaven? In *Shattered Dreams*, Larry Crabb says that we
have to be willing to give up our "happiness" to find the
real "joy" God has in store for us. Many of us are never

willing to do that. When we demand that God answer our prayers right now and exactly as we want them answered, we are keeping God from giving us that which will bring us true joy—a deep and abiding relationship with the one who loves us with an incomprehensible love.[1]

The problem that continued to plague me—my overwhelming need for control—made it difficult to release my loved one into God's care. Was I willing to offer to God those things my happiness depended on? Was I willing to lay my Isaac down? When Abraham showed his willingness to give what he loved most (his son) in blind obedience to God, God taught him one of life's mysteries. He did it for Job. He did it for Naomi. He did it for Paul. He did it for Abraham. And—He did it for me.

During the most difficult phases of the trip, I felt God's presence as never before. It seemed that I was in the palm of His hand, safe from the surrounding storm. When I reached an impasse, God made an oasis in the desert where I received encouragement and refreshment. He gave me joy in situations that were, at times, anything but joyful.

To experience joy in the midst of trials seems like a paradox, but joy and sorrow are actually arms of the same emotion. Real joy is only possible when sorrow is lurking close by. When emotions are raw, the senses are sharpened so that both extremes are acutely felt. To rest under the shelter of God's wing is the closest we can get to the safety of our mother's womb.

God wants us to experience joy. "This is the day the Lord has made; let us rejoice and be glad in it" (Ps. 118:24). The word "joy" is mentioned approximately 165 times in the

Bible. Obviously, joyfulness is important to God. He doesn't expect us, as Christians, to go through our lives with long sour faces like those I saw among the crotchety old church ladies of my youth.

God has a sense of humor and we, who are created in His likeness, have one also. A sense of humor is necessary to survive and thrive during a life-threatening ordeal like cancer. I agree with comedian Bill Cosby, who said, "Through humor you can soften some of the worst blows that life delivers. And once you find laughter, no matter how painful your situation might be, you can survive it." The ability to laugh at one's self in the middle of dire circumstances is stress-relieving and life-promoting. Whether laughter actually plays a role in healing has not been scientifically determined, but few deny its beneficial contribution to well-being.

Physiological and biochemical changes—that can be measured and monitored—accompany a hearty laugh. Scientific studies have shown that laughter lowers blood pressure, increases brain activity, and reduces levels of stress hormones.[2] Whether laughter truly promotes healing might be arguable, but we all know it can improve our moods.

Whether I incorporated a complementary treatment into Jim's therapy depended on particular criteria. The method in question could not present any risk or conflict with his traditional medical regimen. If the method was beneficial (even anecdotally) to a large number of patients, I was willing to give it a try. The use of humor met those criteria. I've never known anyone to die laughing, although I frequently use that hyperbole. Besides, the concept is biblical. "A cheerful heart is good medicine, but a crushed spirit dries up the bones" (Prov. 17:22). Laughter is an inexpensive, readily available form of therapy, so I saw no reason not to use it.

One of the greatest proponents of this holistic method of healing was Norman Cousins, who wrote *Anatomy of an Illness as Perceived by the Patient: Reflections on Healing and Regeneration*. Cousins, a writer, editor, and humanitarian, managed to maintain a positive outlook in spite of a history of serious illnesses. When diagnosed in1964 with ankylosing spondylitis, a disease of the connective tissue, he decided traditional medicine alone would not provide a cure. After much study, he was convinced that stress reduction (along with supplements) would restore his immune system to fight the disease.

"Nothing is less funny than being flat on your back with all the bones in your spine and joints hurting. A systematic program was indicated," wrote Cousins. "A good place to begin, I thought, was with amusing movies." He acquired old classics like "Candid Camera" and the Marx Brothers. "It worked. I made the joyous discovery that ten minutes of genuine belly laughter had an anesthetic effect and would give me at least two hours of pain-free sleep."[3] By employing his own theory, Cousins outlived two serious health crises.

Cancer treatment centers across the country now use some form of humor therapy. The Cancer Treatment Centers of America and Montefiore-Einstein Cancer Center in New York have support groups designed to make the patients laugh. Laughter gives them a sense of control over their disease.[4] Some cancer centers are now using Laughter Yoga, a variation of yoga introduced by a physician in India that is now practiced in fifty-three countries.[5]

If these programs were available when Jim started treatment, I was not aware of them, but common sense told me that a good laugh was therapeutic. When we made our first trip to Houston, a friend gave us DVDs of every humorous movie she could find. These provided entertainment and a distraction from the many problems ahead of us.

The humor therapy programs today are primarily directed toward patients, but the caregiver also needs a healthy dose of laughter to keep her sanity. Had I not been able to laugh and find humor in our situation, I would likely have succumbed to physical ailments produced by stress and tension. My life had become a steady stream of consultations with doctors and nurses, insurance agents, trips to offices, hospitals, and test facilities, waiting for results, coordinating appointments, and making decisions. In a recent study, caregivers had a sixty-three percent higher death rate than a control group of non-caregivers.[6] Stress can take as much as ten years off a family caregiver's life.[7]

To lift my spirits, I chose humorous books which gave a balance to the serious, sometimes depressing books I read about cancer. One of the first books I bought was Barbara Johnson's *Plant a Geranium in Your Cranium,* the light-hearted account of her fight with a brain tumor. The author was no stranger to tragedy and suffering.[8] Her ability to laugh and bring laughter to others was an encouragement to me.

Sometimes Jim and I relied on the manufactured humor in books or films, but many times we found relief in being able to laugh at ourselves. We frequently resorted to gallows or hospital humor that might have been misunderstood by listeners. I've been told that I have a weird sense of humor; my wit has always been a little off-beat, but now it served me well.

This kind of humor must be used with discretion because there are situations in which it is inappropriate and hurtful. I wouldn't walk into a room where someone was recently diagnosed or near death and make an attempt at levity. In fact, I wouldn't make light of anyone else's situation. But laughing with my husband kept both of us from dwelling on the terrible things that were happening. This is an excerpt from an e-mail I sent from the hospital following Jim's prostate surgery.

I knew I was in trouble when I walked into the hospital room. Something was seriously wrong with the feng-shui. My first task was to take Big Ben off the wall and shut him in the bathroom for the night. I have never heard such loud ticking from a battery operated wall clock. While preparing the room so that I might be able to sleep, Nurse Cratchit came through the door. Call me a grammar-snob, but when she used "done" as a helping verb, I immediately wondered if she got her nursing degree on-line. About 1 A.M. she came in, ostensibly to check on Jim, pulled up a chair, and asked him about his lung cancer. (Remember *this* surgery was for prostate cancer.) I was propped up on my elbow in my comfort recliner and Jim was still heavily sedated, but that didn't stop Chatty Kathy.

"My daddy died of lung cancer in '86," she began. "I tell you, that is no pleasant thing to watch. Then my sister-in-law, who was like a mother to me since Mama died in '92, has terrible emphysema but she jest keeps on smoking them cigarettes."

We had the benefit of Nurse Cratchit's rosy outlook for the three nights of the hospital stay. If I hadn't been able to laugh at her, I might have wrung her neck.

God knows that worry robs us of the joy he intends for us to have. When I was younger I was always looking forward to some occasion, if only the weekend activities. Frequently I was disappointed and left waiting for some other happening to focus on. If I wasn't eagerly anticipating an event, I was dreading one. My mother, who called me a "worry-wart," used to say, "The things you worry about never happen." In a perfect example of twisted logic, I proceeded to worry about them—so that they would never happen. The joys of each day were passing me by as I lived in the future.

When we worry, our body goes through physical responses just like those that accompany an actual event. Adrenaline flows and our heart rate increases. Our body reacts just as if we were being chased by a lion, although the thing we're worried about is a fabrication, no more real than the lion. Michel de Montaigne, the famous French philosopher said, "My life has been full of terrible misfortunes, most of which never happened." And, "He who fears he shall suffer, already suffers what he fears."

In *Jesus Calling,* my favorite daily devotional, Sarah Young writes: "Rehearsing your troubles results in experiencing them many times, whereas you are meant to go through them only when they actually occur."[9] Years ago I read Dale Carnegie's classic book *How to Stop Worrying and Start Living* in which he gives similar advice. He wrote his specific worries on slips of paper and deposited them in a desk drawer. When he went back two months later to read them, he realized most of the worries never materialized.[10]

Following Carnegie's example, I made a worry box. When I found myself worrying about some future event or calamity beyond my control, I wrote the worry on a piece of paper, dropped it into the box, and physically removed it from my sight. Before dropping it in, I asked God to work out the problem. I designated one day a month as a worry day, on which I was allowed to open the box and "worry." The process might sound silly, but interestingly, when I opened the box and tried to worry, I realized what a waste of time it was, and went about my day. For worriers, procrastination can be propitious. Like Scarlet O'Hara, put off your worry until tomorrow—when you're stronger.

Learning to live in the moment is one of life's most valuable lessons—and cancer is a demanding teacher. During the cancer journey, I had to take one day at a time because I didn't know what the future held, and I surely didn't have any control over it. Living in the moment, finding pleasure in ordinary events, is a lesson that allowed me to live life to the fullest. Knowing our days on earth are numbered caused me to treasure each one. Jesus tells us, "Therefore do not worry about tomorrow, for tomorrow will worry about itself. Each day has enough trouble of its own" (Matt. 6:34).

I wrote in my journal: "Life is so much sweeter since the cancer diagnosis. God is so good. To live each day seeking His will and abiding in Him really is the only source of happiness and contentment. I am learning, with His help, to live each day to the fullest. I'm even learning to be more flexible and spontaneous (occasionally)."

Another bright spot in the cancer journey was watching our children grow closer to God. The hospital stays offered the rare opportunity to spend time with our daughters as adults. In a reversal of roles, they had the chance to help us and let us depend on them.

Our oldest daughter, after a bitter divorce and twelve years in the world of academia, had moved away from the religion she had been brought up with. After her divorce, she and Jim had a somewhat strained connection, but the imminent possibility of his death hastened the restoration of their relationship. Watching her dad go through cancer treatment not only brought her closer to her father, but also brought her back to the roots of her faith.

Jim's illness followed closely on the heels of his only sister's divorce. They always got along well enough but cancer renewed their sibling bond. Following the example set by her older brother, she turned to God for sustenance during her own battle. Jim says those two events (his sister's and our daughter's spiritual growth) made his journey worthwhile.

All of our family ties were strengthened as we grew in respect for each other. In his testimony Jim says, "I always thought Cyndi and I were close, but the cancer brought us closer." We had time for prayer and Bible study together which we never had when he was working. I appreciated him more when the tasks he routinely performed—pumping gas, paying bills, maintaining cars, taking out garbage—fell to me. Likewise, when he began to feel better, he realized how difficult my job as a homemaker had been. Before he was at home 24/7, he probably thought I spent my days getting manicures and reading fashion magazines.

In *The Life God Blesses*, Gordon MacDonald writes about "disruptive moments" and how they can threaten the soul of a believer.[11] Illnesses that are unexpected, unwanted, and beyond our control are certainly disruptive, yet they provide renewed capacity for spiritual growth—if we turn to the God who loves us and who has allowed this pain to come into our lives.

This growth is another of the blessings of cancer. Disease brings clarity of mind that enables us to see things with a new vision. "Call to me and I will answer you and tell you great and unsearchable things you do not know" (Jer. 33:3). If we listen, God speaks to us as He might not in any other situation. As C.S. Lewis said, "God whispers to us in our pleasures, speaks in our consciences, but shouts in our pain."[12] Or it may be that catastrophic illness makes our hearing more acute.

Cancer took some things away from our family, but God filled the gaps with His presence. There are so many unknowns with cancer. It forces you to turn to what you know and what you can trust, which you soon realize is very little. God led me to a place of acceptance, calmed my fears, and showed me that He would never forsake me. As the lyricist says in one of my favorite contemporary hymns, "When you come to the place that I'm all you have, then you'll find I'm all you need."[13]

Enjoying the Ride

1. Don't be afraid to laugh.
2. If you can't find any humor in the situation, import it.
3. Look for funny movies and books.
4. Surround yourself with upbeat people.
5. Look for nuggets of joy imbedded in the suffering.
6. Make a worry box and only open it once a month.

CHAPTER 8

THE ENDLESS JOURNEY

*It's been an incredible odyssey to make the journey
from a healthy person to someone
with a chronic illness.*

—Karen Duffy

"ARE WE THERE yet?" comes the inevitable question from the back seat en route to grandma's house. When we look forward to the destination, the journey seems interminable.

The passengers on a cancer journey seldom look forward to the end of the journey. More often than not we fear the unknown that awaits us, assuming it will be unpleasant when, in fact, it may not be. Dr. Al Weir likens this waiting to his feelings as a child on Christmas morning. He and his siblings sat at the top of the stairs while their father prepared the movie camera to capture their grand entrance. It never occurred to the children that the surprise at the bottom of the stairs would be something awful, because they knew their father and trusted that he loved them.[1]

"Which of you, if his son asks for bread, will give him a stone? Or if he asks for a fish, will give him a snake? If you, then, though you are evil, know how to give good gifts to your children, how much more will your Father in heaven give good gifts to those who ask him!" (Matt. 7:9-11). We should not fear what God has in store for us when we know His character and believe that He loves us beyond human comprehension.

Whatever awaits us at the end of the road has been postponed, as the long-term survival rates of many cancers are being extended. Every time I turn on the news or pick up a magazine, I read a story about a celebrity who has cancer. I'm not sure if the number is increasing or if I'm more aware—as when I was pregnant and suddenly surrounded by a sea of bulging bellies. Whether or not cancer is rampant is debatable, but people are definitely living longer with the disease. Early diagnosis has increased the success rate of cancer cures. We now treat some cancers as chronic diseases—manageable if not curable.

The problem for survivors and caregivers becomes how to live with the cancer rather than how to die from it. I would much rather have this problem, but it is still a problem. Each time a check-up comes around, I thank God that Jim is still here to get one, but we have had to dig deep into our faith to keep the threat of recurrence from robbing us of the joy in his survival.

Well-meaning friends, in an attempt to mitigate the stress and anxiety we live with, have said, "You know, we all have to go sometime. I could step off the curb and get hit by a truck this afternoon." True. But when you are living with cancer, the truck passes by the house on the hour waiting for you to come outside.

Elizabeth Edwards said in a recent interview that her breast cancer is considered incurable and terminal unless she can live long enough for researchers to find a real cure for advanced cancer.[2] I appreciated her honest and realistic appraisal of her situation. I do wish she had added that "barring a miracle," her cancer is terminal. Many of those diagnosed with incurable cancer are praying researchers will come up with a cure before their time runs out.

You may find this hard to understand; I confessed it to very few people. During the first years of scans, one every three months, I actually was somewhat disappointed when the scans came back clear! I finally figured out that I would have preferred to deal with the cancer than with the fear of the cancer returning. Crazy, I know. I don't live with that constant fear now, but I'd be a liar if I told you it is permanently and forever gone.

It is as if I am living with a giant in my home …. and he is not jolly or green. He invaded my life the day Jim was diagnosed and has been lurking ever since. After I recovered from the shock of his arrival, I thought I adjusted to his presence. But I never, ever forget he is here. I tiptoe around him because at any minute he might awaken, ravenous and threatening. *Will he devour me in one large bite or be satisfied with a little snack to hold him over while he returns to hibernation?* Sometimes he is so quiet; I think he might be dead. Then he stirs, rears his ugly head, and comes back even more ferocious than before.

I know that God must have left the door unlocked allowing the beast to enter. And I know God is able to protect me from the "terror of night" and "the pestilence that stalks in the darkness" (Ps. 91:5-6). Unfortunately head knowledge doesn't take the tension out of life with the giant. This brazen trespasser refuses to be ignored.

The giant's presence in our home creates constant stress. We agonize while waiting for test results. We struggle with life-and-death decisions. We haggle with insurance companies and worry about finances. Only the Word of God drowns out the giant's "fee, fie, foe, fumming." Only the grace of God gives us hope of slaying him.

God strengthens me in the battle with my Goliath just as He strengthened David, the shepherd boy who took on a giant with a sling shot. I don't spend nights weeping in my pillow or days biting my nails. From the day I heard the dreaded word "cancer," I have slept peacefully, relying on His promise in Proverbs 3:24, "When you lie down, you will not be afraid; when you lie down, your sleep will be sweet." Peaceful sleep is a miracle when the monster's snores echo throughout the house.

God has granted me the "peace of God, which transcends all understanding" (Phil. 4:7) because "I cast all my fears upon Him." Yet, while the giant hovers over me, I live with stress. Can I really experience peace and stress at the same time? Are fear and stress different?

Fear is almost always non-productive, immobilizing, and debilitating—a powerful rush of water from a broken dam. God tells us in Isaiah 41:10, "Do not fear, for I am with you." He gives this command because fear robs us of the joy He provides. When the doctor told us that Jim had advanced lung cancer, I was so afraid, I shook for months. I was barely able to get food past the lump in my throat.

Stress is like Chinese water torture with the victim scarcely aware of the first few drips but eventually worn down by the unremitting pressure. Since the giant moved in, I have felt this kind of constant pressure. But stress, unlike fear, can be a positive force. God sometimes allows stress in our lives for our own good. Paul says in Romans 5:3-5, "we know that suffering produces perseverance; perseverance, character; and character, hope." Just as years of physical pressure changes coal into a precious gem, living with the giant is molding me into the person God wants me to be. We only grow when we are stretched, but there is a point of diminishing returns. Too much tension breaks the rubber band or stretches it beyond usefulness.

In college I learned about Hans Selye, the "Einstein of medicine," a famous physician who studied what happens to living things when they are stressed.[3] First the organism experiences the "alarm reaction." I can identify with that. When Jim was diagnosed, I had a three-alarm reaction.

The next stage, according to the theory, is resistance, a period in which the initial stress symptoms lessen. For me, this was adjusting to life with the giant. The intensity of the emotions experienced during the first few months—shaking, not being able to get my breath, weight loss—diminished as I learned to lean on God.

Finally, according to Selye, comes the period of exhaustion, followed by death if the exhaustion continues. As a caregiver I have been exhausted countless times. I lumber along in a state of resistance until some new stressor sends me into the state of exhaustion.

We caregivers must find ways to alleviate the tension or we suffer ill effects. The exhaustion state might not lead to death but it can cause irreversible damage to the body. Selye may have been the "Einstein of medicine" but he didn't know how to recover from this state of exhaustion. Fortunately, Jesus does. "Come to me, all you who are weary and burdened, and I will give you rest" (Matt. 11:28).

God doesn't promise a stress-free life, but He does promise to provide strength and comfort in times of overwhelming pressure. "We have this treasure in jars of clay to show that this all-surpassing power is from God and not from us. We are hard-pressed on every side, but not crushed; perplexed, but not in despair; persecuted, but not abandoned; struck down, but not destroyed" (2 Cor. 4:7-9).

People often comment on my strength in coping with the unremitting pressure of my husband's terminal illness. The strength is not mine. This jar of clay is designed to crack and break, but the grace of God holds it together.

I often sign my letters, "Under His wings," because I clung to Psalm 91 in difficult times. "He will cover you with his feathers, and under his wings you will find refuge; his faithfulness will be your shield and rampart. You will not fear the terror of night, nor the arrow that flies by day, nor the pestilence that stalks in the darkness, nor the plague that destroys at midday" (Ps. 91:4-6).

In her book *The Battle Belongs to the Lord,* Joyce Meyer coins a term for the enemies that threaten us, based on biblical history. God's people in the Old Testament fought their very real enemies—the Moabites, the Ammonites, the Meunites, the Hittites, the Canaanites. Our enemies (or "ites") might not be visible, but they are no less real. We fight the stress-ites, the cancer-ites, the money-ites, or the job-ites. The advice the Lord gave to the Israelites holds true for us today. We can make our battle plan based on what we learn from the Bible.

"When you are faced with a crisis and don't know what to do, follow the instructions God gave Jehoshaphat.

1) Take your position (worship).
2) Stand still and see the salvation of the Lord.
3) Collect yourself.
4) Calm down.
5) Tell your mind to stop figuring out the answer.
6) Turn your focus on God.
7) Open your mouth and sing the songs that are in your heart."[4]

The fourth part of the battle plan has always been difficult for me. Rather than the steel magnolia I would like to be, I fear I am a hothouse orchid. A good strong wind would do me in. Part of how we handle stress is wired into us. To borrow the color code for the national security level warning, I was born at Code Orange and, with the slightest provocation, I move easily into Code Red. I talk fast, move fast, and think fast. My husband, on the other hand, was born at Code Blue. Waiting patiently is not as difficult for him. If you believe in genetic coding, we inherited these differences from our ancestors.

My great-grandparents worked in the tin mines of Wales under danger of a cave-in. After work they probably gathered in the local pub for a few ales and tried to avoid a bar fight. Jim's people were farmers whose daily problems might include the threat of an impending hail storm or rounding up a neighbor's errant cow which had wandered into the bean field. My ancestors were fighters and flee-ers while Jim's were waiters and watchers. No wonder we react so differently to frightening situations.

A caregiver, regardless of his or her innate emotional makeup, experiences "scan-xiety—the tension which builds, particularly among those who have or have had cancer, as they move toward their regular check-up scan."[5]

After you have had cancer and know that bad news is not only possible, but likely, there is never again such a thing as a routine scan. Between two and four weeks prior to scheduled tests, I begin to exhibit physical and emotional symptoms. I become cranky and short-tempered. I am impatient with sales clerks, recorded messages, and careless drivers. I haven't yet, but I want to scream, "What is the matter with you? Don't you know my husband has cancer?" Like Howard Beale in the movie *Network*, I want to open the window and yell, "I'm as mad as hell and I'm not going to take this anymore."

I have more anxiety dreams during the period preceding a scan. Generally the dreams have nothing to do with cancer, so I didn't recognize the connection at first. Even my subconscious mind won't let me entertain the events that really have me worried. I would expect to dream of hospitals and surgeries, but instead I am awaiting my entrance in a play for which I didn't learn the lines. I forget to study for the final exam, or I can't find my locker with the books I need for class. My latest recurring dream: I'm about to graduate but have made no plans for college or a job. For me, the ultimate planner, this is a nightmare.

I am also plagued by free-floating anxiety or the "Under Toad." Years ago, I read *The World According to Garp* by John Irving. The children in the book, when vacationing at the beach, mistook the word "undertow" for "Under Toad." When their father warned them to be careful of the undertow, they quite reasonably thought the pull of the ocean tide was really a nefarious monster lurking beneath the murky water, waiting to pull them to a terrible death.[6] Our family borrowed the term to describe a feeling of impending doom. Pre-scans, I am acutely aware of the loathsome fellow.

I also experience hyperscanxiety. "Hyperscanxiety is the tension following the scan while [waiting] for results."[7] When the results come quickly, as in Houston when we have an appointment on the day following the scans, I have an interesting reaction. I would expect to be immediately jubilant when the news is good, but that is not exactly what happens. I have prompt relief from the Code Red I have generated in the hour at the office, but that is inevitably followed by a let-down, maybe even mild depression.

During the first three months, which I still say are the worst, we had a whole series of bad reports. We never got good news—the result being that I was conditioned to expect bad news. My body responded accordingly. Prior to an appointment I got physically ill, so that by the time we saw the doctor, if he gave us good news, I was unable to accept it as such.

After a few years of good results, my scanxiety was different than it had been in the first year. In terms of the behavioral scientist, gradually the negative response was extinguished by repeated positive reinforcement. By the fourth year of good reports, I was only mildly apprehensive before we met with the doctor. But it only took one "I don't like what I'm seeing here," to take me right back to my intense responses of the early months—shaky hands, weak legs, nausea, and tears. Aha! Then I remembered that the fight or flight response is not conditioned but involuntary. The nervous system is yelling "Danger! Danger!" as the body prepares to save itself. At least now, the after-shocks are not as bad; I seem to recover more quickly.

This feeling surprised me in the beginning, but when I analyzed it, I realized the cause. For four weeks prior to the scans, I operate at Code Orange escalating to Code Red in the last few days. After the scan, I wait, trying to prepare myself for the worst news. The adrenaline pumps into my stomach; physically I am already experiencing the bad news. Then comes the telephone call. "The scans are clear," or "The biopsy is negative." *No cancer? But wait! I'm ready for the battle.* What happens to the adrenaline? I suppose it passes out of the body eventually, but let me warn you, the process takes a few days. Don't get me wrong. I am always grateful for good news, but it takes a while to sink in.

I wonder whether the doctors and nurses are sadistic monsters oblivious to the fact that someone is waiting by the phone for the results that will determine our course for the next months or years. I hate knowing that the scans are read, results are in, but the reports are sitting on a desk or floating around somewhere between offices. Someone, somewhere, knows, but they're not telling us.

Finally when the call is days overdue, I dare to leave the house for a little diversion, and return to a blinking message light. "This call is for Mr. Siegfried. We have your biopsy results. Call the office and ask for Cruella DeVille." Of course, by the time we get the message, the office is closed. If they are not intentionally sadistic, why do they call with the report on Friday afternoon?

All levity aside, God is good and much more patient with me than I am with Him.

Yes, the giant is always present. Yes, I do live at an elevated anxiety level. But, as I explained in the last chapter, God provides an oasis.

How to Live with the Giant

1. Trust God as you would a loving father.
2. Never expect test results on time.
3. Don't compare your ability to cope with that of others.
4. Find someone (other than your loved one) with whom you can share your fears and anxieties.
5. Get out of the house.

CHAPTER 9

RUNNING ON EMPTY IN THE VALLEY OF THE SHADOW OF DEATH

Time is a companion that goes with us on a journey.
It reminds us to cherish each moment, because it will
never come again. What we leave behind is not as
important as how we have lived.

—Jean Luc Picard

ON A CANCER journey there is no return trip. I remembered where I had been, but didn't know how to get there again. No one had scattered bread crumbs along the way.

I'm not sure that I even wanted to return to the old life. Human beings are surprisingly resilient. We adapt, adjust, and accept in order to survive. After the "kidnapping," when my initial terror subsided, I began to identify with my "captors," speak their language, and even make friends with them. What had been completely foreign became normal—even comfortable. Cancer was my Symbionese

Liberation Army and, like Patty Hearst, I fell victim to the Stockholm Syndrome.

From the time I heard the word "cancer," I knew life would never be the same. What I didn't know was that in some ways it would be better. I have adjusted so well to Jim's disease that I have to remind myself how serious the cancer actually is. I sometimes wonder if I exaggerated his condition or magnified his complaints until I re-read the journal and records I kept. When I look at the pathology reports and see the results in black and white, I recognize the reality of a journey that sometimes seems surreal, and realize how well I have adapted to the new normal.

Our new normal is different because we are different. I have given up some of the control I tried so valiantly to maintain in those first years. Still a planner and an organizer, I have at least learned that tests will get scheduled—even if they're not at my convenience. I still have scanxiety and hyperscanxiety, but I'm much better at waiting for appointments and scheduling.

Even if Jim weren't sick, our lives would have changed upon his retirement. For thirty years, the house was my domain. He left early in the morning and never came home for lunch. We shared a bed, but most of the day we occupied two different worlds. My friends whose husbands are about to retire ask me if having him home was a difficult adjustment. For me it was not. When I thought he would be gone forever, to have him around every day was a privilege and pleasure.

Nor did Jim have difficulty making the adjustment. Now he seldom looks at the financial page or calls the office to see what is happening. For someone who planned his life around his occupation, this was a major change—a miraculous change, if you knew the before-cancer Jim.

My routine changed in some lesser, surprising ways. Before cancer, I began my day with oatmeal, a Dr Pepper, and a brisk morning walk. After cancer, I began my day with oatmeal, Dr Pepper, and a thorough perusal of the obituary section in the morning paper. Pre-occupied with Death, I suppose I needed to keep track of his activities. If he was busy in some other part of town, maybe he'd given up camping on our doorstep. Perhaps this development would have occurred without cancer, a natural result of growing older, but my interest coincided with the cancer diagnosis. Religion, survivors, siblings, occupation—I absorbed every detail. *What was the cause of death? Did the deceased linger or go quickly? Where was he being treated? How old was he?*

I thought I was probably the only person to indulge in this morbid proclivity until I confessed my habit to our support group. I found I was not alone, that others did the same thing. I can't explain it. Maybe it's a kind of recurrence paranoia. Strangely, I find it somewhat reassuring to be reminded that life is indeed fleeting and I had better focus on the eternal rather than the temporal.

The further a patient gets from diagnosis without a recurrence, the more likely long-term survival becomes. With lung cancer, the chances of recurrence in the first year are high. Jim passed that mark and then the two-year mark with a few suspicious scans but no new tumors or lesions. In cancer circles we call this NERD—no evidence of recurrent disease. After two years of NERD, we were cautiously optimistic.

In the third year post-treatment, Jim went for a physical to the same internist who had discovered the lung cancer. I answered the phone when his nurse called a few days after the appointment. "Dr. Castellaw wants Jim to see a urologist because his PSA (the blood marker for prostate cancer) is a little elevated," she said in her best "don't-alarm-this-crazy-woman-voice." Failed attempt. I moved immediately to Code Orange.

"What does this mean?" I asked, knowing she couldn't tell me anything that would prevent a full-out body alert.

My reaction was different than it would have been before lung cancer. Rather than complete panic, I now had a more resigned dread of what was ahead. *Here we go again,* I thought. *More tests, more scheduling, more research, more decisions, and more pain and suffering for Jim.*

Jim's PSA was not very high, but once again, our conscientious Dr. Castellaw believed that any change in a former baseline score should be tested, so he ordered a PET and pelvic CT. These tests showed some abnormalities, but only a biopsy would determine whether the tumors were malignant. I had been conditioned to expect bad news from biopsies. As the bell increased the flow of saliva for Pavlov's pup, the word "biopsy" increased the flow of my adrenaline. Bell = food; biopsy = cancer. I think that when the patient is given valium or something equally wonderful in preparation for the biopsy, the caregivers should line up in the waiting room for their fair share. Bible verses are good, but drugs are faster.

Note that the regular scans Jim was having for lung cancer would not have revealed this new irregularity. Anyone with a chronic or terminal disease, understandably focused on that battle, needs to continue to have physicals to monitor for other conditions. If you've had a kidney transplant, you don't want to die from heart disease. If you have been diagnosed with breast cancer, that doesn't mean you won't get skin cancer. I hate to tell you, but cancer, like lightening, does strike twice—sometimes more than twice.

All cancers have in common certain emotional reactions, but prostate cancer is a category unto itself. Dealing with prostate cancer is very different from dealing with lung cancer. People said that after lung cancer, prostate cancer would be a walk in the park. Hardly. Maybe a walk in Central Park at 2 A.M.

Although the prognosis with prostate cancer was better, making it easier for me to accept, the male ego and psychological factors complicated the issue. With lung cancer, we had little feedback from former patients because there were a limited number of survivors. But with prostate cancer, the multitude of survivors had a multitude of opinions about treatment. One contributor to an online support group said, "I'd rather die than never have sex again." Obviously he had never been face-to-face with death.

I wanted the prostate removed if that procedure offered the best chance of eradicating the cancer, and I was willing to risk whatever the side effects of the surgery might be. Fortunately, Jim agreed. Neither of us wanted to add a recurrence of prostate cancer to our very valid worry about a lung cancer recurrence. So the prostate came out.

I heard the wife of a prostate cancer survivor make this seemingly senseless statement: "Prostate cancer is the worst cancer a woman can have." I soon learned what she meant. Our first post-biopsy consult with the doctor who would perform the robotic surgery, opened my eyes to a whole new world where doctors and nurses discuss bodily parts and functions with an abandon I had not encountered in polite society.

The surgeon's right-hand man—a woman in this case— used some interesting slang for bodily functions, terms I seldom heard in my social groups. Both Jim and I repressed nervous chuckles at her use of the vernacular. When discussing possible side effects, "Depends" and "Viagra" are not words you want to hear. We left knowing the surgery would not be the piece of cake we were hoping for.

On the day of the surgery, a conversation with the nurse anesthesiologist exemplified our new normal and how, in an attempt to live with the disease, I had come to minimize its severity. Prior to the surgery, she came in, clip-board in hand, to get Jim's health history.

"Any history of bronchitis or breathing problems?" she asked.

"Oh, yes. He has broncholalveolar carcinoma," I replied as if reporting hay fever.

"What's that you say?"

"Lung cancer."

"How is his lung capacity?" she continued warily.

"Well, he's missing one."

"Any heart problems?" she asked, moving on.

"None," I replied quickly to reassure her. (I wanted him to pass the test.) "Oh. Wait. He does have Wolf-Parkinson-White Syndrome."

"Say, what?"

"Well it hasn't ever really bothered him—just one little episode about ten years ago."

"OOOOK," she said, eagerly turning toward the door. "We'd better call the head man."

The recovery from the prostatectomy was slow and unpleasant. The incontinence continued for several months, the impotence longer. After two years, the doctor was considering more drastic solutions when we encountered a major bend in the road. The year before, Jim had a biopsy of a spot next to his spine which showed up on a PET scan. We were relieved when the biopsy proved negative. Now a year later, when we were considering further treatment for the sexual dysfunction, the latest scans indicated the spot was more active. Another biopsy.

We came back to Memphis to wait for the results. I was drained and exhausted. People who haven't traveled this path just don't understand. Many were congratulating us on Jim's good news. *What good news?* I thought. *That he's still alive? That the doctor thinks this is an unlikely place for a metastasis?* Whatever did I say to make them think that we had good news when the results from the biopsy wouldn't be back for days? They didn't grasp the significance of a recurrence. I prayed the tumor would be benign but prepared myself for bad news and all that would follow. Like Jesus in the Garden, I asked God to take the burden away, and then felt guilty for my lack of strength.

The tumor was cancerous, a metastasis of the original lung cancer. Surgery was not a viable option because of the location near the spine. Grasping for good news, we heard: "The tumor is localized and slow-growing. We can do radiation." No matter how positive I tried to be, I couldn't ignore the obvious. After five years of lying dormant, the cancer was back—or maybe it was never gone.

For five years I wondered whether a recurrence would be more difficult than the initial diagnosis. Now I knew. I can tell you that for me, nothing in this journey, including the recurrence of the lung cancer, equaled the fear, anxiety, and confusion surrounding the initial diagnosis. Then it was as if we had been abducted, thrown into the car, and forced to take a trip, without a map, to an alien country.

Although familiarity made the new path easier to follow, the knowledge I had acquired about cancer caused me to evaluate the latest development realistically. We had been told that BAC was likely to return, but as time passed I was almost able to believe Jim had been completely cured. Now I knew that wasn't true. This metastasis would likely be the first of more.

When we first met with Dr. Rios in December 2002, Jim asked, "What happens if the cancer comes back after you have hit it with all of the drugs in the arsenal?"

Dr. Rios said, "By that time there will be new treatment options." He was right. There were new drugs for advanced lung cancer—Alimta, Avastin, Tarceva. And, thankfully, for us there were new radiation procedures.

Like chemotherapy, radiotherapy has long-lasting, often serious, side-effects. Very simply—beams (photon, electron, ion, and, most recently, protons) are directed to the malignant cells. These rays damage the DNA of the cells causing them to die or reproduce more slowly. Unfortunately, they also can damage healthy cells.)

I was surprised to learn that radiation has been used to treat cancer since shortly after the discovery of X-rays in 1895.[1] Innovations through the years have made it possible to reduce the damage to adjacent organs and healthy cells. The newer radiation available to Jim with the cancer's return had many advantages over the earlier forms of the external beam type he took five years before. One of the major benefits is that patients, like Jim, who have already received large doses of radiation, can undergo this process without further damage to the surrounding organs.

The targeted radiation worked in obliterating the tumor by the spine. The procedure was much more tolerable than chemo and earlier radiation. We were away from home for a few months, but other than fatigue, Jim was feeling so well that it was almost like a vacation.

A short year later, the cancer metastasized again—this time to the bone, specifically to the rib in the area of the original lung surgery. Now we are embarking on yet a different fork in the road with another aggressive chemotherapy regimen. Whether it will be successful remains to be seen.

We are on the road again, but the country is familiar; we know what pot-holes to watch for; and we find comfort in friendly faces. The foe is no less formidable, but we are better prepared to fight him. Now I know that it is possible to live with cancer. I also know it is possible to maintain hope, even when we experience major setbacks. In the words of a Disney song, you have to "Pick yourself up; dust yourself off; and start all over again."[2] I thought I couldn't stand it if the cancer came back. I was probably right. I couldn't stand it, but I "knee-ed it," and God gave me the strength to endure.

HOW TO KEEP TRAVELING WHEN FUEL IS RUNNING LOW

1. Continue to have annual physicals from a trusted doctor.

2. Do not ignore any new or recurring symptoms.

3. Remember that often the fear of recurrence is worse than the actual recurrence.

4. If you lived through the original diagnosis and treatment, you can manage whatever comes later.

5. Hope for the best outcome but prepare for the worst.

CHAPTER 10

LAST MAN STANDING

*Heroes take journeys to confront dragons and
discover the treasure of their true selves.*

—Carol Lynn Pearon

I F EVER YOU'VE watched the television show *Survivor*[1],
you know that not all survivors are admirable. The last
man standing might be the winner, but the end doesn't
always justify the means.

Like the millions of viewers who made the reality show
a success, I have always been drawn to stories of adventure
and survival. When most little girls read the Nancy Drew
mysteries, I opted for *Kidnapped* and *The Adventures of
Huckleberry Finn*. When my teenaged peers were reading
Peyton Place, I was reading about the Hindenburg, the
Titanic, and the Pueblo. Not that I am an intrinsically
melancholy person, but rather that I'm fascinated by tales
of character, courage, and the indomitable human spirit.

In the cancer fight, just as on the television show, the participants share a common goal. Although among cancer patients, there is no competition because there can be more than one winner. When Jim had been ill for several months, I wondered, *when does he become a survivor?* Was he a survivor six months into the disease? A year? Would he become a survivor when the doctors declared him cancer free? Or only when given a clean bill of health? (Lots of luck with that one. That's the only bill a cancer patient never receives.)

According to Webster a survivor is: (1) one who continues to live after or in spite of; (2) a person who has survived an ordeal or great misfortune; (3) a person regarded as resilient or courageous enough to be able to overcome hardship or misfortune.

Just living through an ordeal and coming out on the other side still breathing isn't such a great feat. In 1980 Jim was driving to work in an MG convertible. He slowed to cross a double set of train tracks on a country road where the trees and brush obscured the view. A three-quarter-ton maintenance truck, designed to travel the tracks but not heavy enough to trigger the cross-arm, failed to make the required stop at the crossing, crashing into the side of the MG and pushing it into the path of a train coming from the opposite direction on the parallel track. Jim's car was hit—first by the truck and then by the train which carried it a mile and a half before coming to a stop with the little MG plastered across its front. The car was demolished but, miraculously, Jim lived. He was a survivor—sure enough— but not because he did anything noteworthy.

Similarly, those who outlive a dire medical prognosis might be survivors, but often their survival has little to do with their own effort. To say, "I am a five-year survivor" seems like a claim of personal accomplishment when, in fact, some survivors could best be described as richly blessed or darned lucky. Does the five-year survivor deserve more recognition than the person who dies after a valiant, six-month fight? Is it even necessary to have cancer to be a cancer survivor? Any caregiver who lives through a spouse's diagnosis fits the survivor definition. The length of time one endures and the kind of suffering one experiences are not the measures of a survivor. It makes no more sense to credit someone with survival than to blame someone for death. Both are random events orchestrated by a God whose methods and motives are unknowable. "On a large enough time line, the survival rate for everyone drops to zero" (Chuck Palahniuk).

God is all-powerful and wise. He decides who will live and die—and when—but sometimes the process seems arbitrary and unjust. From my end, an Old Testament kind of deal seems like a more just plan. What a wonderful world it would be if we lived in John Wayne territory where the bad guys died and the good guys rode off into the sunset.

If only we could manipulate God's decisions. "I promise not to gossip, or covet, or kill anyone, if you'll reserve cancer for serial killers and terrorists. I'll keep my end of the bargain and you keep yours." Bad theology, I know, but sometimes the prospect is attractive. Only then could survivors legitimately boast about their survival times.

To think that my way might be better than God's is the ultimate sin of pride. Like Eve, I believe that I can run the world better than God Himself. What arrogance to try to take God's place. Yet, I confess, there are times I'd like to try.

We can't bargain with God, because we can never uphold our end of the bargain. We have nothing to offer Him but filthy rags. We can never understand God's blueprint because we only see it from our side. His purpose is to bring glory to himself. How He chooses to do that doesn't always coincide with our plans, but I have to believe that in the end, His plan will be better for us than any I might devise.

We must be careful to recognize the difference between a survivor and a hero. A hero is a man, or woman, admired for courage, nobility, and strength, a person regarded as an ideal or model. When we talk about a cancer "survivor" what we usually mean is not just someone who lived through an ordeal but someone who did it with courage and pluck.

Not all survivors are heroes and not all heroes are survivors, but they do share many characteristics—determination, tenacity, perseverance, ingenuity, and adaptability. Charles Darwin said, "It is not the strongest of the species that survives, nor the most intelligent that survives. It is the one that is the most adaptable to change."[2] No doubt the cancer survivor shares these qualities with all survivors, but these attributes are not necessarily heroic. What then is it that sets the hero apart from the survivor?

The third Webster definition of survivor comes closest to capturing the essence of the hero-survivor. Anyone resilient or courageous enough to overcome hardship deserves some sort of credit. But what makes a survivor worthy of praise and recognition is not just courage and resilience but the attitude he exemplifies during the ordeal. How much of his character and integrity remains after he has walked through the fires of suffering?

You survived cancer or the ride in the passenger seat. Good for you. Did you learn compassion and humility? Did you come out of the trial refined, shaped, and strengthened? Do you still look for the good in human beings? Was your ordeal a refining process that rid you of impurities? Or did it only bring them to the surface, out in the open for the world to see? Has your suffering been wasted or has it been a springboard for service to others in similar situations?

Living through trials early in life helps develop the survivor mindset. Early setbacks make you secure in your ability to overcome adversity. Our youngest child was diagnosed at age six with a learning disability. In overcoming that disadvantage, she developed the characteristics necessary for survival. By the time she graduated from high school, twelfth in a class of 600, she was confident and secure in her ability to overcome—because she tackled obstacles early-on.

To be a hero-survivor you have to have that same mindset. The survivor says to cancer, "You will not defeat me even if I die. I will maintain my hope and dignity to the end. I won't be embittered or broken or full of hate. I will not only survive; I will thrive."

Elizabeth Edwards is the consummate hero-survivor. The sub-title ("Reflections on the Burdens and Gifts of Facing Life's Adversities") of her book, *Resilience,* says it all.[3] She has the attitude born of the pain and experience of earlier tragedies. Her teenaged son was killed in an automobile accident; she was diagnosed with breast cancer; the cancer recurred around the time that her husband's infidelity came to light in the middle of his presidential campaign. Not only did she experience all that goes along with terminal cancer, she did it in the public eye. She admits the fears she has of leaving her young children but writes, "They will be able to say that I stood in the storm. And when the wind did not blow [my] way—and it surely has not—[I] adjusted my sails."[4] Now that's resilience.

I am not proposing that we stop applauding survival times. Patients and caregivers need to know that miracles happen, that statistics are misleading, that cancer isn't always a death sentence. Length of survival should be celebrated, but every death should remind us that survival is a gift. Hearing from someone who beat the odds gives the newly diagnosed encouragement and hope.

Hope is essential to survival. "Man can live about forty days without food, about three days without water, about eight minutes without air, but only for one second without hope."[5] This quote of unknown origin is, of course, hyperbolic but the sentiment is accurate. Trying to maintain the right balance between hope and realistic expectations is one of the most difficult aspects of living with a chronic or serious illness. We are driving on the edge of a deep precipice, sometimes so close that I can see the rocks sliding down into the canyon. In the passenger seat, I press my foot on the non-existent brake to prevent our fall. I sometimes hang on by a thread, but if I didn't have hope, I would open the door and throw myself into the first river we crossed.

Hope is "a feeling that what is wanted is likely to happen" or "desire accompanied by expectation" (Webster's New World College Dictionary). If I subscribed to that definition, I would be traveling in a state of hopelessness. What I wanted to happen initially was for Jim's tumor to be benign. What I wanted next was for the surgery to remove the entire tumor. What I wanted next was for him not to have prostate cancer. What I wanted next was for the cancer never to recur. Obviously, I didn't get what I wanted.

How can we who are living with catastrophic disease preserve the expectation of the fulfillment of our heart's desires when things don't turn out the way we want? In *Jesus Calling*, Sarah Young writes, "Hope is a golden cord connecting you to heaven. This cord helps you to hold your head up high even when multiple trials are buffeting you."[6]

Our hope as Christians is based on more than the fulfillment of our wants and desires. Our hope is based on the promises God gives us. "So God has given both his promise and his oath. These two things are unchangeable because it is impossible for God to lie. Therefore, we who have fled to him for refuge can have great confidence as we hold to the hope that lies before us" (Heb. 6:18 NLT).

When our path is full of obstacles and we stumble and fall, God encourages us, holding us up by that golden cord, pulling us ever closer to Himself. "We can rejoice, too, when we run into problems and trials, for we know that they help us develop endurance. And endurance develops strength of character, and character strengthens our confident hope of salvation. And this hope will not lead to disappointment.

For we know how dearly God loves us, because he has given us the Holy Spirit to fill our hearts with his love" (Rom. 5:3-5 NLT).

Hope makes suffering bearable. When our journey takes us to the valley of the shadow of death, when the doctors have run out of options, we have to look to God for a miracle, or focus on the miracle that will occur at the moment of death.

Jim and I have seen so many miracles, but I know that a complete healing may not be in God's plan for us. The experts tell us that once a cancer has recurred outside the area of its origin, a cure is not possible. So my hope is in the Lord. He is "my refuge and underneath are [His] everlasting arms" (Deut. 33:27). Whether Jim is cured or not, I hope I will continue to praise God and thank Him for His goodness.

We are hopeful that the latest regimen of chemotherapy will knock the cancer out once and for all. This kind of hope, based on the efficacy of the treatment, is available to anyone—Christian or not—as any cognitive therapist will tell you. But if the cancer ultimately destroys Jim's body, it cannot destroy the hope we have in Jesus Christ. In Him, the battle is already won.

TOOLS FOR SURVIVAL

1. Choose your heroes and emulate them.
2. Develop a survivor mindset.
3. Fix your eyes on the eternal, not on the temporary.

4. Remember where you are headed.
5. Put your hope in that which will never fail.

CHAPTER 11

LEAVING A ROADMAP

It is not down on any map. True places never are.
—Herman Melville.

THE QUEST TO find meaning in suffering is age-old. When Job, a good and faithful man, lost everything important to him, he and his friends sought to explain his undeserved plight. Four thousand years later, we react the same way to devastating circumstances, attempting to find a logical reason for what befalls us. Although the demand for fairness is universal, life is not fair. The righteous and innocent suffer along with the evil, and sometimes we never see a reason for it. Whether God causes suffering or allows it is an interesting question for debate, but the answer doesn't matter much to the afflicted. When the journey is difficult, travelers need direction.

Jim's cancer diagnosis caused me to face the problem of pain. I searched and researched in an attempt to understand suffering and the character of the omnipotent God who allows it. As a result, I'm on much firmer ground now than I was in the early parts of the journey. There are aspects I will never understand, mysteries that will remain just that, but because God has revealed Himself in countless ways, I am absolutely certain He is involved in the details of our everyday lives and that He provides strength and encouragement to those suffering physically and emotionally.

While I don't have all the answers, I know one reason God allows us to suffer is so that we can help people in situations similar to our own. "Praise be to the God and Father of our Lord Jesus Christ, the Father of compassion and the God of all comfort, who comforts us in all our troubles, so that we can comfort those in any trouble with the comfort we ourselves have received from God" (2 Cor. 1:3-4). Sharing a burden with fellow sufferers makes the journey easier.

Jim and I were desperate for conversation with other couples facing serious illnesses but we weren't able to find any group or organization that met our needs. Our family and friends provided support, but we wanted to talk with people who knew first-hand what problems come with life-threatening disease. When we couldn't find a Christian support group in our metropolitan area, we decided to start our own, calling it: f.a.i.t.H, facing an illness through Him. We had no idea how to establish the group or how to conduct the meetings. Six people attended the first one, which we promoted in the church bulletin. When they arrived, we weren't really sure what to do with them.

Through trial and error, we were able to come up with a program to help patients and caregivers face the problems of catastrophic illness. Being the recipients of help from God and loving friends, we wanted to provide the same kind of help for others. As is often the case, the people we were trying to help ended up helping us. Reaching out to others took our focus off our personal problems.

Although f.a.i.t.H is unapologetically Christian, some of the attendees are not. The purpose of the group is not evangelism, but sometimes when non-believers observe faith at work and see the strength and courage of the believing members, they are drawn closer to God. They come seeking physical and psychological healing, but go away with healing of the spirit which is ultimately most important. The group is a way to point people to the great physician, the only real hope in situations they face.

Such was the case with Fereydoon. Ferris, as his American friends called him, was an Iranian Muslim who fled his native country in 1986 for political reasons. One of his work associates who knew about our group asked if we would talk with him.

When we met Ferris, he was recovering from open heart surgery, during which the doctors discovered that he also had tuberculosis and lung cancer. In spite of his multiple health problems, he welcomed us warmly into his home. Although he was weak, he was eager to talk to us about his ordeal and overwhelming triple diagnosis.

Ferris was never able to attend a meeting, but the rest of the group prayed for him, as Jim and I continued to visit and develop a friendship with him and his wife. A year after our first meeting, Ferris made a public profession of his faith in Jesus Christ. Three days later, he went into a coma—never to speak again. His funeral service was held at a Baptist church with hundreds of his Muslim friends attending. The next time we see Ferris will be at the throne of Jesus.

Mark came to our monthly meetings for two years. We never asked his religious affiliation but assumed he was a Christian, as was his wife. When he was at home with hospice care, very near death, Jim and another of our members paid him a visit. His wife met them at the door.

"There is something you should know," she whispered. "Mark is Jewish. Some of the influential members of that community are with him now, saying their goodbyes. I'd love for you to come back later to talk with him." Jim and Jules went back that afternoon and several more times that week. Before he died, Mark accepted Jesus Christ as the Messiah and will spend eternity praising Him.

Sometimes we became discouraged when few people showed up for a meeting. But we soon learned that the number in attendance is not directly proportional to the efficacy of a support group. Some of our most meaningful meetings were with the smallest groups. One of the families we grew closest to in the early years was from Venezuela. Their little girl, Marisella, was a patient at St. Jude Children's Research Hospital where she was in long-term treatment for sickle cell anemia. Thousands of miles away from home, they were desperate for connection. Despite the language barrier, we formed a lasting relationship with them.

People are drawn to the group for the same reasons we were led to start it. They are seeking connection, information, support, and direction during a time when they don't know where to turn. During the past seven years, we have counseled over 150 people—most with cancer but some with sickle cell anemia, kidney disease, auto-immune disease, and interstitial pneumonitis. We have welcomed Protestants, Catholics, Jews, and Muslims—all of us sharing the bond of catastrophic illness.

Friends ask me if ministering to people with serious illnesses is depressing. It is not. Cancer reminds me that we are mortal beings and that all of us—even those who are cancer-free—are terminal. The courageous people we meet are an inspiration to us.

You may not be equipped or inclined to start a support group, but there are many ways you can give back to the community that has helped you. The method you choose is not only dependent on your natural gifts and personality, but also on where you are in your personal battle. If your loved one is in remission, you may have more time than if you are busy with daily care.

Not everyone is comfortable in a group or visiting hospitals, but anyone can be an encourager. If you make yourself available, God will provide opportunities for you to share what He is doing in your life. You don't have to be a fount of wisdom to be effective, but you must be sensitive and empathetic. I can pass on some tips from my own experience.

Don't spout platitudes and Bible verses. When I was so distraught over Jim's illness, well-meaning visitors offered the usual words of wisdom in an effort to comfort me. I took these in the spirit they were given, fully appreciating the intent and concern of the speaker, but they offered little hope.

When someone said, "Trust in God. Everything will turn out all right." I thought, *What? Do you have a crystal ball? What's your definition of 'all right'?* If they said, "God never gives you more than you can handle," I thought, *Really? I'm afraid He's overestimated me.* Or, the worst, "If you have enough faith, Jim will be healed." That platitude gave me one more burning coal to add to the heap already on my head. If he wasn't cured, the fault would be my flimsy faith.

When talking with someone who is in the midst of crisis, remember Aesop's tale of the boy drowning in the pond. An old man came by and saw his predicament and began to lecture him about his carelessness and stupidity. The boy hollered, "Throw me a rope now and give me advice later!"[1] The suffering man needs a rope, not unsolicited and often poor advice. Once the drowning man feels more secure, he will be ready to listen to counsel.

First give the caregiver or patient a chance to talk so that you can determine where they are on their journey. With the newly diagnosed, don't give them more information than they need. Too much information to a new patient is like giving a child more information than he can handle about sex. When I was expecting our third child, our six-year-old asked me, "Where does the baby come from?" Being an enlightened mother of the boomer generation, I sat down to answer her in great detail. When I was finished, she looked at me blankly and said, "I meant, which hospital will you go to?"

Let your friends talk or cry without offering a discourse on your own ailments and problems. Don't frighten them with horror tales about your personal journey or fall into the one-upsmanship game. "My son's cancer was worse than yours," or "I have suffered more than you can imagine."

If you don't know what to say, don't say anything. Just listen. Sometimes with the f.a.i.t.H. group, it seems as if we are doing very little—a monthly meeting, visiting local cancer centers, sending an e-mail prayer list, visiting the hospital, and mailing notes and cards. But it is enough. People in crisis just want to be heard and to have their pain acknowledged. Being able to talk with someone, with no fear of judgment, is often the best therapy.

Pay attention to the ravings of a person in the throes of a physical or spiritual battle. If she is already in a relationship with God, chances are God has something of value to say to her. If personal interaction is difficult for you, send a card to let the family know you are thinking of them. It may not seem like much, but when you have been on the receiving end of those small kindnesses, you know the value.

Some survivors and caregivers use the knowledge and wisdom acquired during their fight by becoming advocates for a particular disease. Every catastrophic disease organization needs volunteers to promote awareness, spearhead activities, and raise money.

You may want to join the War on Cancer. Once we received Jim's diagnosis, I naively believed the doctors would know exactly how to accomplish a miracle cure. Like most Americans I thought we had made great strides in cancer treatment. I was shocked to learn that much of treatment protocol is determined by trial and error.

There are as many theories about the cause and resolution to cancer as there are cancers. Most of them are interesting but not really relevant to the patient. Scientists spend a lot of time theorizing about the causes of cancer. Unfortunately, the time spent theorizing doesn't directly translate to a longer life span for the afflicted.

I haven't become cynical, but I have learned that the success of the War on Cancer has been greatly exaggerated or possibly greatly misunderstood. Since Richard Nixon declared the War on Cancer in 1971, the death rate from some cancers has declined—notably breast, colon, and prostate. Much of that improvement is because of early diagnosis. Deaths from lung cancer, liver and bile duct, melanoma and pancreatic cancer are rising. Although the progression has been slowed somewhat, metastatic disease of any kind is nearly always fatal, and we still don't know how to stop it.[2]

Those of us affected by lung cancer have been waiting for someone famous and influential to take up the banner, but so far no one has risen to the occasion. Seven years ago when Jim was diagnosed, Kara Kennedy, the daughter of Ted Kennedy, was also diagnosed with the disease and treated in New York City. Reportedly her prognosis was good but we never hear a word spoken about that event. Yet we frequently are reminded of her brother's bout with cancer years earlier. People are less-forthcoming about lung cancer, perhaps because of the mistaken belief it is self-inflicted. No one deserves lung cancer—or any other disease.

Dr. Rios did much of his early research in the treatment and prevention of AIDS. He told us that lung cancer needs a political push like the one AIDS research got in the 1980s and 1990s from the activism of the gay community. Breast cancer research received a similar thrust from women's groups.

I don't know what powerful interest group can do that for us. Peter Jennings couldn't. Dana Reeves couldn't. Even the Shah of Iran couldn't. Paul Newman didn't. Each time I see one of these prominent people whose private battles are thrust in the public eye, I pray they will bring more money for cancer and greater awareness of the problems cancer patients and caregivers face. Because of the high death rates from lung cancer, we don't have many survivors to espouse the cause. Maybe a caregiver, impassioned by the loss of a loved one, can fill the gap.

Ted Kennedy, Patrick Swayze, Elizabeth Edwards, and Farrah Fawcett have been open about their cancer battles. I applaud them for their courage in sharing with us and pray their plights will draw much needed attention to the problems of securing unapproved drugs for terminally ill patients. The costs of treatment are soaring; we need someone to plead our case with government and drug companies. "Congress now has an opportunity to address this problem thanks to Senator Sam Brownback (R-Kansas) and Representative Diane Watson (D-California), who introduced the Access, Compassion, Care, and Ethics for Seriously Ill Patients Act". This act would give terminally ill patients access to drugs that have not yet been approved by the FDA.[3]

If politics, activism, or volunteerism doesn't appeal to you, God may find another way for you to contribute. Illness is transforming. You will be changed, and in the hands of God those changes can be positive. Your journey might lead you down a path that you wouldn't otherwise have explored. Suffering can give birth to increased creativity. The writer has something to write about; the singer sings with deeper feeling; the artist finds new methods of expression; the speaker has an enriched platform.

If it weren't for Jim's cancer, I would never have considered writing for publication. When we traveled to Houston for treatment, although I was computer illiterate, I began (with the help of my daughter) e-mailing to keep a few friends and family members apprised of his condition. As I searched for strength and direction from God, the letters became unedited outpourings of my innermost feelings.

I was astounded by the responses of the recipients.

"Your e-mail meant so much to me."

"I forwarded it to my sister who has breast cancer."

"I could identify with your feelings."

"I appreciated your honesty."

What began as a mode of communication became an outlet for my emotions, and ultimately a way to connect with the readers on a deep level. Initially I was reluctant to open myself up to possible criticism and rejection, but cancer gave me new purpose and boldness. "What I tell you in the dark, speak in the daylight; what is whispered in your ear, proclaim from the roofs" (Matt. 10:27). Over the next five years, the e-mail list grew as we made thirty-five trips to Houston. With God's leading and the encouragement of a writer's group, I have written this book and several articles directed toward caregivers.

God doesn't waste our suffering. He really can bring good from the most dismal situations. When we come to an obstacle in the road, He either clears the way or allows a U-turn. God didn't cure my husband of cancer, but He did lead me to an alternate path. What I thought was a catastrophe took me to a new and fulfilling purpose—to write and tell others what God has done in my life. "And we know that in all things God works for the good of those who love him, who have been called according to his purpose" (Rom. 8:28).

I didn't want to make this journey, but my life is immeasurably better because I did. I heartily recommend our travel agent, tour guide, and driver. He has taken us down new roads—me as a writer and Jim as a speaker—allowing us to tell anyone who will listen about God's faithfulness and the ultimate hope we have in Him. Our plans may have been thwarted by cancer, but God's plan was better than anything we could have devised on our own. "'For I know the plans I have for you,' says the Lord. 'They are plans for good and not for disaster, to give you a future and a hope'" (Jer. 29:11 NLT).

WORDS FOR THE WEARY TRAVELER

1. Don't waste your suffering.
2. Reach out to others.
3. Find a support group where you can contribute, or form your own.
4. Become an advocate for what you are passionate about.
5. Be open to what God has planned for you.

THE CAREGIVER'S GPS (GOD'S PROMISES FOR THE STORM)

1. Philippians 4:6-7 "Do not be anxious about anything, but in everything, by prayer and petition, with thanksgiving, present your requests to God. And the peace of God, which transcends all understanding, will guard your hearts and your minds in Christ Jesus."

2. 2 Corinthians 12:9 "'My grace is sufficient for you, for my power is made perfect in weakness.' Therefore I will boast all the more gladly about my weaknesses, so that Christ's power may rest on me."

3. 2 Corinthians 4:16, 18 "Therefore we do not lose heart. Though outwardly we are wasting away, yet inwardly we are being renewed day by day. So we fix our eyes not on what is seen, but on what is unseen. For what is seen is temporary, but what is unseen is eternal."

4. Matthew 6:34 "Therefore do not worry about tomorrow, for tomorrow will worry about itself. Each day has enough trouble of its own."

5. Psalm 91:4-6 "He will cover you with his feathers, and under his wings you will find refuge; his faithfulness will be your shield and rampart. You will not fear the terror of night, nor the arrow that flies by day, nor the pestilence that stalks in the darkness, nor the plague that destroys at midday."

6. Proverbs 3:24 "When you lie down, you will not be afraid; when you lie down, your sleep will be sweet."

7. Romans 5:3-5 "We can rejoice, too, when we run into problems and trials, for we know that they help us develop endurance. And endurance develops strength of character, and character strengthens our confident hope of salvation. And this hope will not lead to disappointment. For we know how dearly God loves us, because he has given us the Holy Spirit to fill our hearts with his love."(NLT)

8. 2 Corinthians 4:7-9 "We have this treasure in jars of clay to show that this all-surpassing power is from God and not from us. We are hard pressed on every side, but not crushed; perplexed, but not in despair; persecuted, but not abandoned; struck down, but not destroyed."

9. Hebrews 6:18 "So God has given both his promise and his oath. These two things are unchangeable because it is impossible for God to lie. Therefore, we who have fled to him for refuge can have great confidence as we hold to the hope that lies before us." (NLT)

10. Deuteronomy 33:27 "The eternal God is your refuge, and underneath are the everlasting arms. He will drive out your enemy before you, saying, 'Destroy him!'"

11. 2 Corinthians 1:3-4 "Praise be to the God and Father of our Lord Jesus Christ, the Father of compassion and the God of all comfort, who comforts us in all our troubles, so that we can comfort those in any trouble with the comfort we ourselves have received from God."

12. Jeremiah 29:11 "'For I know the plans I have for you,' says the Lord. 'They are plans for good and not for disaster, to give you a future and a hope.'" (NLT)

13. Isaiah 61:1, 3 "He has sent Me to bind up the brokenhearted...and provide for those who grieve in Zion—to bestow on them a crown of beauty instead of ashes, the oil of gladness instead of mourning, and a garment of praise instead of a spirit of despair. They will be called the oaks of righteousness, a planting of the Lord for the display of His splendor."

14. John 14:27 "Peace I leave with you; my peace I give you. I do not give to you as the world gives. Do not let your hearts be troubled and do not be afraid."

15. Isaiah 43:2 "When you pass through the waters, I will be with you; and when you pass through the rivers, they will not sweep over you. When you walk through the fire, you will not be burned; the flames will not set you ablaze."

16. Psalm 147:3 "He heals the brokenhearted and binds up their wounds."

17. James 1:5 "If any of you lacks wisdom, he should ask God, who gives generously to all without finding fault, and it will be given to him."

18. Psalm 55:22 "Give your burdens to the Lord, and he will take care of you. He will not permit the godly to slip and fall." (NLT)

19. Psalm 119:50 "Your promise revives me; it comforts me in all my troubles." (MSG)

20. Psalm 121:1-2 "I lift up my eyes to the hills—where does my help come from? My help comes from the Lord, the Maker of heaven and earth."

21. Psalm 119:28 "My soul is weary with sorrow; strengthen me according to your word."

ENDNOTES

Chapter One: "Kidnapped"

1. Henry Smith. *"Give Thanks,"* Integrity Music, 1986.
2. Corrie ten Boom, *The Hiding Place,* (New York: Bantam Books, 1974), 198-200.
3. Don Moen, *Give Thanks: Give Thanks with a Grateful Heart,* Integrity Music, 2004.

Chapter Two: "A Jerky Start"

1. Shel Silverstein, *A Light in the Attic,* 1st ed. (HarperCollins, 1981), 90.
2. Stephen Jay Gould, "The Median Isn't the Message," *Discover* 6 (June 1985), 40-42.

Chapter Three: "On the Road"

1. Dr. A. L. Gill, *God's Promises for Your Every Need,* (Nashville, Thomas Nelson, Inc., 1988).

2. Devra Davis, *The Secret History of the War on Cancer*, (Basic Books, 2007).

Chapter Four: "The Road to the Crazy House"

1. Marc Silver, "Grief Before Death," *Cure* (Fall 2007), 68-72.
2. Elizabeth Kubler-Ross, *On Death and Dying*, (Scribner, 1997), 51-123.

Chapter Five: "A Detour—Exploring My Faith"

1. John Piper, "Don't Waste Your Cancer," www.desiringgod.org (February, 15, 2006).
2. Idor Sadger, *Recollecting Freud*, (University of Wisconsin Press, 2005), 127.
3. Lee Strobel, *The Case for Christ*, (Zondervan, 1998).
4. C.S. Lewis, *Mere Christianity*, (Harper, 2001).
5. Patrick Glynn, *God: The Evidence: The Reconciliation of Faith and Reason in a Postsecular World*, (Three River Press, 1999).
6. Francis S. Collins, *The Language of God—A Scientist Presents Evidence for Belief*, (Free Press, 2007).
7. Al B. Weir, M. D., *When Your Doctor Has Bad News*, (Grand Rapids, Michigan: Zondervan, 2003), 61.
8. Ibid., 97.
9. Paul Francis Webster, "I'll Walk with God," Alfred Music Publishing,1954.

Chapter Six: "Fuel for Body and Spirit—God's Provisions"

1. Brian Greene, *The Fabric of the Cosmos*, (New York: Random House, 2005), 81-115.

2. Ibid, 178-196.

Chapter Seven: "Streams in the Desert"

1. Larry Crabb, *Shattered Dreams*, (Colorado Springs: Waterbrook Press, 2001).
2. Marshall Brain, "How Laughter Works," *How Stuff Works, www.health.howstuffworks.com* (April 1, 2000).
3. Norman Cousins, *Anatomy of an Illness as Perceived by the Patient: Reflections on Healing and Regeneration*, (New York: W. W. Norton & Company, 1979), 43.
4. Ula Ilnytzky, "Illness a Laughing Matter," *Memphis Commercial Appeal*, (November, 30, 2008), A11.
5. Nygal, "Review: Laughter Yoga," *www.cancerdirectory.com* (December, 2008).
6. R. Schulz and S. Beach, "Caregiving as a Risk Factor for Mortality: The Caregiver Health Effects Study," *Journal of the American Medical Association*, Vol. 282, No. 23, Dec. 15.
7. "Impact of Caregiving," *Careconnection.com*.
8. Barbara Johnson, *Plant A Geranium in Your Cranium*, (Thomas Nelson, 2002).
9. Sarah Young, *Jesus Calling*, (Nashville: Thomas Nelson, 2004), 17.
10. Dale Carnegie, *How to Stop Worrying and Start Living*, (New York: Simon & Schuster, 1944).
11. Gordon MacDonald, *The Life God Blesses*, (Nashville: Thomas Nelson, 1994), 23-43.
12. C.S. Lewis, *The Problem of Pain*, (San Francisco: Harper Collins Publishers, 1940), 91.

13. Gary Mathena and Ed Kee, "Lean on Me," 1981.

Chapter Eight: "The Endless Journey"

1. Al B. Weir, *When Your Doctor Has Bad News*, (Grand Rapids, Michigan: Zondervan, 2003), 63.
2. Elizabeth Edwards, interviewed by Katie Couric, CNN Cable News Network, 3/22/07.
3. "Stress—an Overview," *www.eapcism.com/starttrainingstress.asp.*
4. Joyce Meyer, *The Battle Belongs to the Lord*, (New York: WarnerBooks, 2002), 26.
5. Community Dictionary, *www.definition-of.com.*
6. John Irving, *The World According to Garp*, (New York: Random House, 1998), 531, 32.
7. Community Dictionary.

Chapter Nine: "Running on Empty in the Valley of the Shadow of Death"

1. "Radiation Therapy," *Wikipedia—The Free Encyclopedia*, *www.en.wikipedia.org.*
2. Jerome Kern/Dorothy Fields, "Pick Yourself Up," 1936.

Chapter Ten: "Last Man Standing"

1. "Survivor," CBS Reality Show, 2000.
2. http://thinkexist.com/quotes/charles_Darwin.
3. Elizabeth Edwards, *Resilience*, (New York: The Crown Publishing Group, 2009).
4. Sandra Sobieraj Westfall, "We had, I Believed, a Great Love Story," *People Magazine*, May 18, 2009, 62.

5. http://thinkexist.com/quotes/survival.

6. Sarah Young, *Jesus Calling*, 9.

Chapter Eleven: "Leaving a Roadmap"

1. Jack Kent, *Fables of Aesop*, (New York: Parents' Magazine Press, 1972), 12-13.

2. Sharon Begley, "We Fought Cancer...And Cancer Won," *Newsweek*, September15, 2008.

3. Steven Walker and Ronald Trowbridge, "How the Senate Can Help Ted Kennedy," *The Wall Street Journal*, Wednesday, June 11, 2008, A23.

RESOURCES AND RECOMMENDED READING

(IN ADDITION TO THOSE LISTED IN END NOTES)

1. ACOR—Association of Cancer Online Resources, www.acor.org
2. f.a.i.t.H, facing an illness through Him, www.faithsupportgroup.com
3. The Cancer Crusade, cawthons@thecancercrusade.com
4. Lynn Eib, *When God and Cancer Meet* (Wheaton, Illinois: Tyndale House Publishers, Inc., 2002).
5. Brenda Ladun, *Getting Better, Not Bitter* (New Hope Publishers, 2002).
6. Dr. David Jeremiah, *A Bend in the Road* (Nashville: W Publishing Group, 2000).
7. Dr. Jerome Groopman, *The Anatomy of Hope: How People Prevail in the Face of Illness* (Random House, 2003).